"A beautiful book. No one could fail to be moved by this intensely personal, deeply compassionate work, full of pathos and joy."

—**Andrew Linzey**
Director of the Oxford Centre for Animal Ethics

"Red is a story many of us who love dogs will deeply relate to and find inspiration in. Ed Sellner explores the beautiful geography of our intimacy with companion animals and the graces they offer to us with loving attention. Read this book to fall even more in love with the gifts animals can bring to our lives."

—**Christine Valters Paintner**
author of *The Soul's Slow Ripening*

"Dog lovers! Animal lovers! We all see and experience the Divine spark in the animals that share our lives. . . . Ed Sellner captures the profound lifelong effect on his heart and soul that his dog, Red, has left. He shares a true Celtic Christian experience of the Divine, one which can only be known through a sensitive relationship with animals."

—**Bishop Cait Finnegan**
Celtic Christian Church

"With clarity and insight Ed Sellner weaves threads of theological and personal reflections for those facing the loss and grief of a beloved pet. . . . The reverence and awe offered through the stories and wisdom of this book provide a notable source of healing and spiritual guidance."

—**Terry Shaughnessy**
Spiritual Director and Retreat Director

"This is a beautiful book—and a book that teaches us why beauty is holy. Grounded in both the simple beauty of the life of a good dog and the overflowing riches of the Christian tradition, *Our Dog Red* illuminates the true and central place of animals in our pursuit of a deeper understanding of the mysteries of suffering and love in God's beautiful, beloved creation."

—**Colleen Mary Carpenter**
St. Catherine University

Our Dog Red

Our Dog Red

A Small Token of Remembrance

EDWARD SELLNER

RESOURCE *Publications* · Eugene, Oregon

OUR DOG RED
A Small Token of Remembrance

Resource Publications
An Imprint of Wipf and Stock Publishers
199 W. 8th Ave., Suite 3
Eugene, OR 97401

www.wipfandstock.com

PAPERBACK ISBN: 978-1-5326-9566-7
HARDCOVER ISBN: 978-1-5326-9567-4
EBOOK ISBN: 978-1-5326-9568-1

Manufactured in the U.S.A.   08/16/19

Apprehend God in all things,
for God is in all things.
Every single creature is full of God
and is a book about God.
Every creature is a word of God.

 —MEISTER ECKHART

… to see the face of the Crucified in the faces of
suffering animals.

 —ANDREW LINZEY

Contents

Introduction

Her full name was Red Moon Goddess, named after the color of her hair and after the name her mother bore. We called her Red for short, but because of my love for the moon, I sometimes remembered her full name with a smile. "Red," in Russia, means "beautiful," I discovered on a pilgrimage to Russia years ago with a friend, and on my travels to China, I learned the same color was associated with beauty and its transforming power. So it seems appropriate that I had spontaneously and early on come to refer to her often as "Beau," short for Beauty. She was that, above all else: beautiful physically, a cocker spaniel with bright red hair and a chest of snowy white, as well as beautiful temperamentally, gentle, gracious, and, in her mature years, elegant, resembling in many ways Lady from Walt Disney's "Lady and the Tramp."

With her beautiful red coat, I always associated Red with being an *Irish* dog, a smaller Irish setter perhaps, although she was listed officially in her pedigree papers as an "American Cocker Spaniel." She *was* Irish to some degree, I think, not only because she liked Irish whiskey, at least when my younger son Daniel offered it to her one St. Patrick's Day, but because she loved to socialize, to be at the center of any party or gathering we had in our house on Princeton Avenue in St. Paul. She would greet every person arriving at the door, always with her tail wagging, even, for the most part, when she encountered total strangers. My wife, JoAnne, and I often commented to ourselves how, if they were robbers, Red would probably, if anything, kill them with kindness, welcoming them in and wagging her tail while they took anything of value. (The only time, I remember, Red wasn't friendly was one Christmas eve, the night I brought a vagrant into the house to give him food from our dinner table, and Red, with her hair literally standing on end, growled viciously at him in a way I'd never seen or heard before. Perhaps she knew something that wasn't obvious to me! JoAnne in the meantime had grabbed the purses in our entryway—as if she had a similar intuition!)

At our numerous parties, however, Red was not always there just to please people, of course, or to make them feel at home, but to check out what goodies she could snatch from the table when no one else was looking. This was the reason she was seldom invited back to my mother-in-law's house—following the time we heard Rita shriek that Red had somehow managed to climb to the middle of the dining-room table, and was devouring the main course, roast beef.

For a variety of reasons, then, Red loved our parties, social events, and family gatherings. She filled the room with her presence, with a *puella* energy that Carl Jung associated with youthfulness in a woman. She always was a puppy at heart, even in her last days when, although sick with a disease that we could not diagnose, she ran lickety-split down the sidewalk with a friend of mine running with leash in hand, trying to keep up with her.

Red was Daniel's and my dog, *our* dog. Together we had driven to a Wisconsin farm to find her; together we had raised her; together we were with her when she took her last breath, dug her grave behind the house, and buried her ashes beneath a stone Celtic cross which became her marker. Although my older son, John, loved her, he was already in high school when she came into our lives. JoAnne loved her too, but with a little less outward enthusiasm, shall we say, particularly when Red chose to defecate in the backyard, so close to JoAnne's beloved flowers.

Dan and I, however, loved her as a full family-member. I would joke: "She's your sister," and he'd reply, "You're her grandpa; I'm her dad." Red always belonged to the two of us, although as Dan became a teenager, she increasingly spent more time with me. It was I who housebroke her, fed her, washed her, took her for haircuts and veterinarian visits; and, yes, even though Dan had signed an agreement before we brought her home to take care of her, it was I who cleaned up after her in our backyard. She reciprocated the attention, frequently joining me in my study, sleeping at my feet, as I worked at my computer, writing one book after another. This was what I loved about her, my companion in writing, my muse.

This book is the story of Red, a dog that changed Daniel's and my life profoundly. When she died on Good Friday, the day associated with Jesus's death, the synchronicity of that timing forced me, a theologian, to ask the questions, "Why?," "Why now?," and "What am I suppose to learn *from this*?" Her death evoked in me other questions too about the significance of animals, whether they might have souls and live beyond this life, what they can teach us, what sort of God created them—and us. This book is an attempt at responding to those questions. Her dying, when she did, also led me, eventually, into the field of an emerging theological discipline, "animal theology," begun with Andrew Linzey in Oxford, England, and defined simply as "a theology concerned with the suffering of animals." Years after Red's death, when I presented a paper on the Celtic saints and their kinship with animals at the first international conference sponsored by the Oxford Centre for Animal Ethics which Linzey had founded, I started with the acknowledgement, "I wouldn't be here except for my dog, Red." I trace my journey into teaching courses in animal theology at St. Catherine University, of investigating spirituality, art, and ethics as they relate to animals, and my writing a book on the Celtic saints and animals back to her. Red has been my teacher, my spirit guide, my soul friend.

Stephen Webb writes in his book, *On God and Dogs: A Christian Theology of Compassion for Animals*, "Although animals can be traded, processed, and consumed, I want to insist that, from a theological perspective that takes pets seriously, animals are more like gifts than something owned, giving us more than we expect and thus obliging us to return their gifts."

This book about Red is an attempt to identify, as I work through my grief, what she taught me about God, and to name those qualities of hers I want to incorporate into my own life and personality. In some small way, it is my gift back to Red for the gift of herself, for the love she gave Dan and me so freely and generously. It is a small token of remembrance.

ONE

New Puppy

Although I had had puppies as a child (my first one, a cocker spaniel named "Peppy," given to me by my father when I was five years old, and a second one when I was ten, a chihuahua named "Spotty"), it was Daniel's idea to get a dog. He had wanted one for years, he said, and when his best friend Marty got one, he wanted one too. But his parents were resistant, until finally, with his persistence, JoAnne and I decided that at this point in our lives we could accommodate his wishes. So Daniel and I set out one Sunday afternoon in early fall across the border into Wisconsin where two farms had advertised puppies for sale. We had initially wanted a Westie, a small white dog I associated with Scotland, and we were going to look for one on the first farm we stopped at. There we found five new Westie puppies, but, as Daniel said later, "they were cute, but nothing distinctive about them that caught my eye." So we moved on to the next farm that was selling American cocker spaniels. One in the litter of tan-colored puppies immediately caught our attention: a beautiful female cocker with *red* fur, playing with her brothers, seemingly dominating them as we watched. She was the assertive one, and both Daniel and I immediately made our choice based on that quality, and her own beautiful color, red.

So there we were, the new puppy lying on a blanket on the floor between Dan's legs, as I drove back across the Minnesota border, stopping at one point to let her out to relieve herself. So small, there at the side of the road, almost lost to sight in the weeds bordering a corn field, with its tall stalks of corn. When we brought her home that first night we placed her gently in the clothes' basket in the living room with a radio, playing soft music, by her side to give her the impression of not being alone. The next morning, however, when I came down to look for her, I found Red, having knocked over the basket and climbed out, wandering the house, whimpering at her new surroundings, probably wondering where her mother and her brothers were. Lonely then, she would find much love in a household which highly valued her.

Because of her color, it seemed only natural to call her "Red," a name that she quickly realized belonged to her. She adapted well to her new surroundings, but her surroundings had problems adapting to her puppy teeth. She seemed to need to gnaw on everything—to the detriment of furniture, shoes, sandals, socks, whatever. All of this activity, of course, had to do with teething, a natural process that lasts from three to six months for a puppy, but a process not always appreciated by a puppy's owners. Still, there was humor involved, as the cartoon JoAnne gave to me, cut out of magazine a short time after Red had arrived, revealed: showing two couples sitting in a room, facing each other, talking, with the furnishings a bit worse for wear, showing jagged edges on many items. The one couple saying to their guests, "Yes, we have a new puppy."

The other major adjustment, of course, was house-training, something that Dan, JoAnne, and John left for me to do. House-training, the experts say, needs consistency, patience, and positive reinforcement, with the goal of instilling good habits in the dog, and a loving bond with one's pet. My recollection, from my dad's example, however, was to instill fear of punishment in the puppy so that she would avoid having any accidents. Being a type-A personality, I expected Red to be trained in a very short time. I didn't know any better, is my excuse, in recollecting my treatment of her, but I do recall Bobbie, my sister-in-law telling me not be so impatient nor spank Red when she had an accident. In retrospect, I did not intend to be harsh or cruel, but I realized that I was overdoing it when I walked into the living-room one evening where Red and the rest of family were gathered and she let out a shriek and ran from me! *That* response certainly got my attention! While the others laughed, I was filled with a stab of guilt that Red would be so afraid of me, and I felt so bad for her! But, so many people, including my dad, said that one must have dominance over a dog if she or he was to learn to do the right thing. I should have listened to what Bobbie said about patience, consistency, and moderation as the true and loving path for a vulnerable puppy.

I was also impatient with Reddy on our walks. Again, I look back and am astounded at my insensitivity! She was a little puppy, and I expected her to keep up with me, not loitering or investigating the surroundings. She had what I interpreted as a stubborn streak, and I had to train her to see me as "the master." While she would stop and sniff and want to investigate everything (curiosity was certainly one of her attributes—and she was a puppy after all), I had my own agenda which was to keep moving on, while pulling on her leash when I felt I had to. One time an elderly woman in another neighborhood, standing outside in her front yard, came over to see the new puppy, pet Red, and give her a treat. All fine and good, I thought, a nice gesture—except on future walks Red wanted to stop at the house every time we went by it—even when the woman was not outside! I became impatient and started pulling on the leash. Red was not to be moved! She did a sit-down strike, and lay on the sidewalk, demonstrating her civil disobedience. Well, that did not set right with me, so I gave her a nudge with my foot on her posterior. Still, she would not move! I had to pick her up and carry her until we could no longer see the house. Again, in retrospect, I realize I should have been more understanding of a puppy's appreciation of a woman's love on her walk, but I mistakenly had that notion that dogs must respect their master, and that fear was the most effective learning-tool. Oh, the guilt and remorse I still carry as I look back on those early days with Red.

Thank God she was house-trained in a short amount of time, and thank God I grew to enjoy our walks as she grew older. I let go of my hurried stance at getting the walk over with so that I could get back to "important things" that needed to be done. This was the routine our family had gotten into: busyness, activities, school meetings, JoAnne with her stressful work and myself with classes days and some nights, as well as administering various programs at the college. What I learned as Red matured was that the walk in itself was a very valuable part of my day. With her, I could unwind a bit (after the first block when Red held the leash in her mouth initially and sped away, dragging me along), and enjoy the seasonal changes (except of course, living in Minnesota, the one that lasted six months out of the year). But it was Red who taught me to slow down, to begin to follow her inclinations and curiosity, and really see much more than I had been aware. She was the one who taught me, as they say, to "take time to smell the roses." And, as I told my friends after a while with Red, she was the one who took *me* for a walk—leading me, straining on the leash, especially if she saw a squirrel or rabbit. She was, after all, a "cocker spaniel," and was naturally drawn to chase them when she saw them. She loved the walks, and sometimes when I told her, "no, we can't go," she would look stricken in ways that were hard to bear. Dan remembers when he'd take her for a walk the sound of her nails scraping the pavement as she pulled on the leash, and how exhausted she seemed to be at the end of their time together.

Her walks with me became part of a routine in which we covered certain blocks, leading down to the river that flowed majestically a few blocks away on River Road in St. Paul. This neighborhood near the Mississippi river consisted of mostly mansions, owned by the well-off, with homes set back far from the sidewalk we walked on. The only time Red and I had what I considered to be a near-fatal encounter was, as we walked by one of the larger homes, I saw a large black lab, without a leash, run from the family seated outside for a picnic and head straight for Red and me. Red, of course, seeing it as her immediate responsibility to protect me hurled herself toward the approaching dog, barking loudly to demonstrate her determination. This, of course, only incited the huge black dog to go for her. I grabbed Red in my arms, and yelled loudly at the family to call their dog, while they seemed inclined to ignore the impending confrontation. Finally, in what seemed an eternity, they yelled, and the dog turned back without killing the two of us. It was a very close call with Red trying to attack the black demon as I attempted to shield her from harm. That was a walk that sent terror through me, and so we avoided THAT neighborhood for some time, with me—if we did go down that block—always looking beforehand to see if the black lab was out and about—without a leash!

This incident with the black lab may be connected somewhat with Red's fierce anger, years later, when Dan brought home a black lab puppy. He had been hinting to JoAnne and me about wanting *another* dog. Both of us had subtly suggested, *no*, absolutely not! This was when Dan in high school was seldom seen with any regularity in the house. So, we thought that we had made it clear that another dog would not be welcome. One evening, however, we came back from an evening out with friends only to hear sounds of a whining puppy in the bathroom downstairs. I opened the door, and there she was, a black lab puppy probably about three or four months old, looking up at me. Red, of course, moved quickly from curiosity to outright hostility as I picked the puppy up and held her on my lap in the kitchen. She growled fiercely as I tried to comfort the poor waif, abandoned evidently by my son without telling either of us, his parents, of his decision to bring her home. Red was not accepting this intruder, and seemed intensely jealous as I held and petted her. No way, she seemed to say, this is my territory, my house, and I am not about to share the wealth!

We had to separate the two, with the new puppy seeming to ignore Red's hostile response as if to say, "What's up? What's the big deal?," and Red becoming increasingly vociferous, barking loudly in the puppy's face. JoAnne took Red upstairs while I waited for my younger son's return with the puppy in my lap. "I appreciate your compassion for another dog," I told him when he sheepishly entered the kitchen and realized we had found the newcomer in the bathroom where he had left her. "But," I said, "it's obvious Red will not tolerate another puppy in the house—nor will I. After all, you are seldom here anyway, and I am not about to train another puppy, however dear, and take on that added responsibility. You have to return her to her owner." Dan, hearing Red's growling and barking upstairs, and seeing the determination in my eyes, relented. She was gone the next day. And Red had gotten her way, as she had a right to do. (The sweet puppy did find a home with one of Dan's friends who gave her the name "Shell," and whom Dan saw frequently. So, in that regard, all ended well.)

As the months passed with Red becoming so much a part of our family, we watched, Dan and I, our puppy growing into a dog with her own personality and character traits. One of the characteristics of Red that emerged fairly soon, once she had become acquainted with our house and its environment (a large Dutch Colonial with a backyard, enclosed by a white fence, and a front yard with evergreens to the side and bushes by the front door) was her sense of needing to protect us. She identified herself in that role, and although always friendly to people who came to our house as guests, she did see the need to bark at those who went by on the sidewalk. She would stand in our family room looking out the large windows which because of their length reached from the ceiling to the floor, allowing her to observe whatever and whomever went by. If she saw a stranger, she would bark loudly to warn us of the danger we faced! This quality, of course, is shared by many dogs; it's part of their genetic make-up, bred over centuries and millennia to be watch-dogs. But Red really took it upon herself to be the one with the responsibility of protecting us; *she took it personally.* Although the mail carrier was a regular, Red still didn't trust the man, and would bark long and loudly until he had deposited our mail in the box, left our property and could no longer be seen in the neighborhood. If, as very infrequently happened, a black garbage bag or any other foreign object was blown by the wind into our yard or across the sidewalk, she was outraged by this strange object too. And, of course, if other dogs appeared in the vicinity, she knew she must rid us—and herself—of their intrusion into HER territory.

Another trait was her curiosity, manifest in the walks we took, as I have mentioned; what I came to refer to as her "nose-i-ness," her need to investigate almost everything, it seemed, that crossed our path. This trait, I think, was certainly related to her capacity for wonder. How could every stone be worthy of sniffing, every clump of grass a source of fascination? Why did some trees or flowers require a more thorough examination? Some of it certainly was related to what Virginia Woolf calls "the realm of scent," a "world of perception nearly closed to us, though open to the nostrils of a spaniel in nearly unthinkable abundance." Surely this scent, related to nature as well as the excrement of other dogs which had preceded us, opened a whole new world to Reddy of which I was not aware. Still, there was much more to her curiosity than that. She wanted to know the neighborhood first-hand, and she wanted to see and smell everything she could. It is why she responded so joyously to the word, "walk," and the phrase, "do you want to go for a walk?" The very suggestion elicited such excitement, expressed in her tail wagging rapidly from side to side, that there was no going back on such an enticing opportunity! Anticipating this wondrous event, she couldn't stand or sit still, but would spontaneously jump up and down, to the point that I had to grab her collar and make her stop, just to get the leash on; and, once it was on, she'd push the door open with her nose. Down the street, often with the leash in her mouth, she would run. "Walk" was one of those magical words that elicited from her such joy and enthusiasm that at times to avoid a scene I would spell the word out if I was in conversation with others: W-A-L-K. Other words that elicited great enthusiasm were related to her adventures on her walks, such as "rabbit," or "squirrel." There was also, of course, the word "treat," and even "mouse"—after the time when I staggered into the kitchen in the morning for my first salvific cup of coffee to start the day and she promptly and proudly dropped a baby mouse, still alive, at my feet! That was one gift I did not appreciate! But even this was part of her curiosity; rather than kill the mouse, she seemed happy in what she had found, curious about the furry little tike, and wanting to share her joy with me—who was now, even without coffee, wide awake.

Her curiosity was especially manifest the first Christmas she had with us when still a puppy, she seemed to be spending so much time near the tree. At first we thought it was the bright lights and various decorations that attracted her, but soon noticed that she lingered more constantly with a particular wrapped gift my sister, Marybeth, had sent her. It contained, we discovered when the package was opened Christmas eve, a certain "treat" which Red had smelled, I'm sure, the preceding days. We humans, however, did not know its contents, and marveled at the inquisitiveness Red showed the package, and her evident frequent need to guard it. Happy she was that first Christmas eve when she was given it to her unwrapped! "At last," she seemed to say, "it's mine!"

This "nose-i-ness" and desire to explore was related closely to Red's joy of living. For her, every day was a new beginning that she would welcome with anticipation. The moment in the morning I opened the door to her kennel in the kitchen which she slept in at night, she would spring out, ready for another day. She went immediately to the backdoor to be let out, and upon relieving herself, began exploring the backyard in case any new creatures had invaded it. In the summertime, she also needed to check the numerous raspberry bushes bordering one side of our fence. Dan remembers how she would "pluck" them off the bushes, carefully putting her teeth around each one she intended to consume without damaging any of the plants on which they grew. Then, before she came inside for her breakfast, she even took time to smell a few of the numerous flowers JoAnne had planted. Red was a dog with a high aesthetic appreciation of beauty in all its forms.

She also had a wonderful love of play which had initially drawn both Dan and me to her when we noticed how much she was enjoying herself with her siblings on the farm, climbing all over them and being the dominant one. But, after we had brought her home, we noticed this same trait of great happiness in her when she was interacting with us humans. Some of this was probably instinctual—as many breeds, including cocker spaniels, were taught over the centuries to retrieve certain items for their human owners. Many still have this innate disposition to "fetch," to chase after objects, pick them up in their mouths, and bring them back. For Red, chasing a ball that Mel, JoAnne's father, would throw across the yard was an activity she totally enjoyed. He would often pretend to kick it one way and then actually send it in another direction, trying to fool her. She would, nonetheless, pluck it up with great happiness, once she had recovered it, and brought it back to him and laid it at his feet for another round of fun. (In his last days when cancer had slowed him down, she would just sit in the chair beside him, and lay her head on his lap, offering comfort to a dying man.) She would also love running madly in circles in the backyard—to get her exercise? to impress her watchers? to just have fun? She had a terrific sense of humor too while playing. She knew, for example, when Dan and I were pretending to fight with each other that we were playing, and she'd bark at both of us. She also enjoyed our yells and comments as she ran with Dan or others chasing her. Trying to catch her, she would run all the faster, happy to be free and the object of our chase. Dog experts tell us it is important for puppies to play because it helps them develop social and physical skills that they will need for the rest of their lives. Red certainly developed them from an early age, but what was most amazing was observing how much fun she had at play, and how much joy, in turn, she brought others. A phrase she loved to hear was when I would tease her (and she knew she was being teased) with the words, "Do you want to play?" With me repeating them to watch her joyous reaction, "Reddy, do you want to play? Do you want to play?" Her tail would begin wagging fiercely and she'd circle around my chair, wherever I was sitting, and then head for the backdoor to our backyard—where she would run in circles, ever wider, joyously barking with each step she took. Playing renewed her spirit, as it did ours; from her we learned of its importance in every creature's life.

Red also was a smart dog, adapting spontaneously as a puppy to her new environment, responding to our various efforts at communicating with her. Certain words which I've already mentioned were a part of the vocabulary she learned quickly. Dogs, in general, try to understand human language and do—some hundred or more words, according to studies. They cock their heads and pay attention, a look in their eyes of concentration on what they do not initially understand, but are determined to do so. They try—which is more than a lot of humans attempt to do. Red was in that mode, from the first day we had brought her home. After a few months, though, Dan began taking her once a week to an obedience school, desiring to increase her vocabulary for her sake and ours, and teach her some discipline. Words like "sit," "stay," "come." Such actions, tied to these words, were rewarded with a "treat" (another word that she especially responded to). Sometimes Dan's aunt Bobbie would go with the two of them to these classes. During one of these sessions when Bobbie was there, the instructor had started the training associated with the word "heel." This act included slightly kicking the dogs to get them to stop pulling on the leash and instead follow the human at their side. However, when Bobbie saw this kicking happening to Red, she said to Dan, "Okay, that's it—no abusive or cruel treatment of Reddy. We're going!" (Bobbie felt strongly about the treatment of puppies, as I mentioned earlier.) It may have been the end of Red's obedience training, but she had learned a lot, judging from how she followed Dan's orders when he said certain words. When I tried to do the same, she would just look at me and then keep going. There was *no heeling* on her walks with me; she pretty much did what she wanted to do. Clearly, it was *her* walk, and I grew eventually to perceive her as my guide, leading *me* to new awarenesses.

This assertiveness on her part was related intimately to her enthusiasm for trying new adventures. She seemed to look for reasons to wag her tail. One of her early adventures with Dan and me was visiting the farm, outside of Breckenridge-Wahpeton, where my mom now lived with her second husband, after the death of my dad. Clark had been a farmer all his life, and Mom had joined him on his farm following their wedding. When we took Red there for the first time, I am sure there was a sense of deja-vu since she had come into the world on a farm in Wisconsin. But she had been a puppy there, and probably not at all capable of exploring that environment. Now, arriving as we did one weekend and letting her out of the car, she looked around as if this was a whole new world to conquer. She took off lickety-split in every direction, heading for the various buildings where Clark kept his tractor and other farm equipment to the chicken coops with the cackling of hens as she approached, to the fence that surrounded the house and fields. Red loved what she saw, and wanted to continue her adventure, though we had to watch her to not go near the road where an occasional car and pickup would speed by on its way to town. That first night, when my mother prepared a wonderful supper of pork chops, mashed potatoes, sauerkraut, salad, and corn on the cob, Red expected to share in the bounty. Yes, she loved the food of humans, and was often fed from the table at our house. This night, she thought, would be no different, and I did slip her pieces of pork and a bit of potatoes. Corn on the cob, however, she had never tried. When I offered her a bite off the cob, she took the whole thing in her mouth, and proceeded to chew the kernels rapidly from its top down. Clark, of course, was not impressed with this display of enthusiasm, nor with the almost immediate result that when the corn went in one end of Red it almost immediately discharged at the other! While I was quickly grabbing paper towels to stop the disaster, Red wanted to keep eating this delight that she had never had before. Did I mention how much Clark was outraged at his meal being interrupted with this unpleasantry? Yes, I immediately stopped Red's happy meal, grabbed her, and took her outside to finish the cob. But her tail never stopped wagging at this wonderful surprise.

Perhaps two of Red's most significant qualities were her patience and gentleness with us in the family and those who took care of her. There are many dogs who, if cornered or threatened or unhappy with their owners' treatment, defend themselves, growl fiercely, bare their teeth, and even bite. Red did not. Dan and I do not remember her ever doing so. She never responded to us with anything but acceptance; not growling or biting when we were disciplining her or angry at something she had done. She took it with a patience that Martin Luther King would have identified with his own teachings on satyagraha, a method with the aim of arousing the conscience of oppressors in order to bring about social change based upon principles of courage, truth, and non-violence. Red had already demonstrated on one of our first walks as a puppy, as I've related, her own ability to protest non-violently the injustice I was showing her by laying down on the sidewalk and refusing to move. As she grew older, along with her patience, a beautiful gentleness emerged, that quality of being kind and tender-hearted. Her groomer, Carol Juelfs, was a wonderful woman whose love of dogs was demonstrated by caring for dogs in her home as well as grooming hundreds of dogs a month. She told me after Red died how patient Red was all while she cut her hair. "But," Carol added, "her most outstanding quality was her gentleness. She loved people, and, as is true of American cockers, she was more friendly than English cockers who are bred to be hunters and are more serious. Red wanted to bond, and she was so trusting—compared to other dogs whom I have known." Others observed this about Red too. Veterinarians who cared for her over the years and whom she got to know for exams, shots, teeth-cleaning, and other procedures often commented to me how patient and gentle she was with them—despite, as we will see, her intense fear of being in their offices as she grew older.

All of these qualities, ultimately, I think, were related to her unconditional love. Love that attracted love in return. This love was manifest in her always being willing to forgive, to put any past grievances behind her, to live in the moment with love and kindness, and move on. It was reflected in her hospitality, her enthusiasm for new and old friends, excited to see them, wagging her tail in anticipation. The Irish poet William Butler Yeats once said that "There are no strangers here; only friends who have not yet met." Red, without knowing it, seemed to believe that, expressed by her welcoming people to our home and making them happy to be greeted by such a friendly animal. (Well, except for my Christmas eve guest!) With Red, all of these qualities were related to her tremendous capacity for love; for Red, always love. Red was the epitome of *love*—forgiving, hospitable, joyful, manifest daily in her wagging tail at the door and her expectant face, expressing joy and happiness.

Thank God, her early days of fearing me had changed into bonds of genuine affection. Red was like my "shadow," Dan said. He remembers her always sitting in the blue Lazy Boy chair in the living room, lying next to me on my right side. Her joy in human companionship, expressed in her wagging tail. Always until her last days, but even then, when recognizing a friend, she would wag her tail—not as wildly as before, but a wag nonetheless.

The love was reciprocal between Red and me. As JoAnne once told me humorously (I think), "She's the woman you always wanted in your life—besides your mother; always waiting at the door, happy to welcome you home; never blaming you for anything; forgiving you whatever you had done; slobbering you with kisses."

JoAnne may have exaggerated a bit, but she had a point—as was her wont.

TWO

Spirit Guide

Life is filled with transitions, some major, some minor, but they affect us all, humans and animals alike. After Red had joined our family, our sons John and Daniel began moving into adolescence, a new phase of life for them (and their parents!) with its own trials and uncertainties. John, our older son, finished grade school and went on to Cretin-Derham Hall, becoming increasingly busy with academic and social activities, and a part-time job at an Italian restaurant in our neighborhood. He initially had not been enthused about bringing a dog into our home, but, as Dan recalled, he "literally came to love Red, although he'd never admit it." Dan was in his last days at nearby Nativity grade school where he had made lifelong friends, Marty, Mark, and Michael. Dan remembers that despite his times away from home with them, on his return he would find Red at the top of the steps where she often slept and how she'd run down to meet him, offering him her love which, of course, was reciprocated. Sometimes too when he came from school, he could see her standing at the window, looking out, always looking—and then disappear like a flash to the door, wagging her tail, and waiting for his entrance. He would open the door and she'd dance around him, so happy to see him. His love for her is obvious in the pictures that were taken of the two of them early on. Dan is always smiling broadly with Red at his feet or being held, enjoying Dan's loving attention.

While our boys were adjusting to their changing circumstances, their parents had their own transitions to deal with. JoAnne, a lawyer working for the state legislature, had a career that kept expanding in responsibilities. Especially when the legislature was in session, she often spent long hours, sometimes extending into the night, with weekends filled as well. Red perhaps was not so much an intimate part of her daily life, but a constant presence when she was home. Obviously she did not always appreciate what Red left among her flowers or, needless to say, the times when Red would nip at her heels. But she did greatly appreciate Red in other ways, happy that our dog brought Dan so much joy as well as contributed to her husband's happiness. She also appreciated how much her dad, Mel, loved Red and found enjoyment playing with her, especially during the time he was increasingly sick with a cancer.

My responsibilities as professor in the theology department at the College of St. Catherine in St. Paul also grew. In addition to teaching undergraduate and graduate classes and administering pastoral ministry and graduate programs, I worked for a number of years as chairperson of the National Association for Lay Ministry (NALM), an organization dedicated to promoting lay leadership. That took me to meetings and conferences in various cities in the States, from Boston to San Francisco, New Orleans to Chicago, San Antonio and even Rome itself for an international conference I helped plan and promote. My frequent travels seem to have affected Red, since JoAnne told me upon my return from one of my trips, "Red misses you when you're gone. She mopes around and seems lost." Reassuring words that Red loved me, but also an awareness that made me sad when I left for my trips.

Though each of us then had our own challenges and transitions to deal with, Red had hers. She was maturing too—from a puppy with short legs and a large stomach to a mature dog with strong legs and a slim chest. Besides physical changes as she aged, there were the emotional ones as well. All dogs certainly experience the same stages of life that humans do, only at a more rapid pace that seems to vary according to size: puppyhood ends between six and eighteen months when adolescence starts; adulthood emerges between twelve months and three years; senior years begin between six and ten years—sometimes later. Studies and observations show puppies can be more demanding, certainly energetic, and, as we saw with Red, more prone to want to chew on anything. On her first visit to JoAnne's parents' home she had chewed through the wires connecting their new television set (not a happy introduction for them!). Adult dogs, usually, with the proper love and affirmation, become more self-assured, able to read human emotions and respond accordingly, and especially eager to express their energy through play and exercise, a characteristic mentioned already about Red. By the time they're seniors, dogs, like humans, begin to take things slower and hopefully more comfortably if their owners help them and not make the same demands as they might with younger dogs. (Red did slow up a bit, as we all do, when she got older.)

Reddy made her own adaptations as she matured and became increasingly a more significant part of our family and our daily lives. Holidays changed the pace a bit, times certainly more exciting, disrupting the ordinary routine. Christmas, of course, was one of the most exciting times for her and for us. JoAnne took over the kitchen, baking a wide variety of cookies and sweets. (On her father's Hungarian side of her family, there was a pastry cook whose talents she seems to have inherited.) I was in charge of Christmas decorations inside and outside the house. My dad had inspired me when every year he would climb the shaky ladder, leaning against the exterior of our home in Wyndmere, North Dakota, and place the colored lights around the borders of the house and a bright star over the front door. I had inherited the star and the practice, happily decorating the exterior of our home on Princeton Avenue. I also would go out to purchase a live tree each year, always a tall Fraser fir. It was my responsibility to put up and decorate the tree, although Dan usually was the one who helped me carry it inside and put it in the stand. Red always was excited when these activities began, meeting us at the door when we brought the tree inside,

and watching as the lights were placed and lit, and then each orna-
ment carefully hung in its branches.

Christmas eve was when JoAnne's family and relatives gathered around our table for a sumptuous dinner, sometimes joined
by my mom and Clark, and my sister Marybeth. It was always a
fun time with my family when they could be there, but especially
with JoAnne's sisters and brothers, their spouses and children, her
mother Rita and her father Mel, arriving with their boxes of food
for the meal and Christmas gifts. These gifts would be opened in
the living room after the dinner of prime rib, mashed potatoes,
sweet potatoes, peas and corn, and, of course Rita's specialty, cran-
berries. Mel brought the bread he had baked that everybody loved.
In the midst of the doorbell ringing to announce each carload of
people and gifts, Red would be there, at the door, to give her own
special greetings, barking excitedly and wagging her tail. She obviously also looked forward to our sitting down at our large dining
room table filled with wonderful scents of delicious food. Oh, I
think this was the high-point of Reddy's year when people, myself especially, were giving her morsels under the table where she
waited expectantly. If the waiting was too long, in her estimation,
she would bark for attention. After the meal and the gifts began to
be handed out and opened by each person, Red would move from
one to another, hoping, something might be for her! Aunt Bobbie
never disappointed, always bringing Red something, as well as a
gift from my sister, Marybeth, which she brought or mailed if she
couldn't be there. All of this became part of a wonderful pattern
surrounding the Christmas holiday.

One year, though, there was an explosive, as it were, digres-
sion from the usual routine. Joe, my brother-in-law married to
JoAnne's sister, Carol, had brought Jason, his son from a previous
marriage, to the dinner. A teenager at the time, Jason, wanting
to be helpful, decided on his own to fill the fireplace with logs. I
mean, fill! I was always in charge of the fire, and knew from some
years of experience how many to put in. Certainly no more than
three, maybe four at the most. Jason, however, piled at least ten

logs, on top of each other, in a pyramid as it were, and then closed the glass doors!

We were all still at the table, finishing dinner, when Red, being a guard dog, after all, began to bark excitedly in the living room where the fireplace was located—and which I could not see from where I was seated at the table. But I did become aware of her loud barks. As I got up to check on Red, and rounded the corner, I, and everyone else, heard what sounded like an explosion. Which it was! An explosion of shattering glass doors, overheated by the burning logs. I went running into the room, which Red was running from, her tail between her legs! Thank God she wasn't hurt but certainly terrified—as was I! Shattered bits of glass covered the rug. But, again, thank God nobody else was in the room when the doors exploded. Granted, I did have very hostile feelings the rest of that evening, as I cleaned the rug of its pieces of glass, and attempted not to act on my feelings of wanting to throttle Jason. That was one evening, in particular, which stands out in my memory: Jason, the fire, exploding glass, and my watchdog Red who tried to warn us of impending disaster.

This Christmas eve incident, while upsetting at the time (and somewhat humorous in retrospect), helps me now realize the importance of Red. In this instance, she was a sentinel or watchdog of imminent doom, but even more so a guide to being alert to what she saw or felt. (Remember the vagrant whom I had invited in on another Christmas eve, and Red's vicious reaction to him, fiercely growling and barking in a way I had never heard before.) Dogs can be like that, with their extrasensory abilities that come from their ears, smells, perceptions. Developed through the centuries to be watchdogs, if we pay attention to them, they can awaken us to things of which we have no idea or awareness of happening. Recent studies also reveal that dogs are more intuitive than we thought, often attempting to tell us non-verbally, through barking or whining, something that may be amiss or some dynamic we are overlooking. Like the very talented pig in the movie, "Babe," it is helpful, as the farmer did, to become aware of their attempts at communication.

As I look back on my life with Red, I recognize that she was there for me as I was making my own transition into midlife, helping me in ordinary ways, but also in certain memorable ways in recognizing changes my life was calling me to make. Our walks, often daily, were the more ordinary ways of discernment. As I have already alluded to, Red loved to chase any squirrels or rabbits that we encountered on our walks, always running to the end of the leash and trying to drag me to join in the chase. Her instincts of hunting, as a cocker spaniel, took over as she attempted to capture them and to bring them back to me with them, she hoped, clamped between her teeth. That was her intent—always frustrated by the leash! But there were also the walks in which both of us could relax and observe our surroundings, and the changing seasons. This was when our walks became a form of prayer, Reddy leading the way, my guide to greater awareness of my own surroundings, and especially of my inner self. Like a spiritual guide, she offered me time for reflection that I probably wouldn't have had, with so many other things going on. She also offered me a reassuring presence that led me to a growing awareness of new directions and possibilities in my life.

Different traditions identify spiritual guides in diverse ways. There are, of course, a wide variety of significant *human* spiritual guides from the starets of Orthodox Christians to the Jewish rabbi to the shaman of Native Americans to the Hawaiian kahuna. Among Celtic Christians the Anamchara or soul friend was seen as both a spiritual guide in this life, but also one who, like hospice ministers today, helps another make the transition to the next. Besides human guides, there are angels whom Judaism, Christianity, and Islam, among the major religious traditions, recognize as guardians in this life and guides to the next. Ancient Egyptians believed in the jackal-headed god Anubis who led the dying to the underworld; in Brittany, it is Ankou, a shapeshifter who appears in many guises, including as a tall thin man wearing a long, hooded cloak or as a skeleton with a scythe (a Father-time figure). Birds, such as eagles, owls, cranes, and ravens in various traditions, especially in the Celtic, are also commonly known to assist the flight of the soul from the body.

Among sensate creatures, perhaps dogs are the most well-known as faithful companions to humans in this life. This is why, for example, on so many tombs in medieval churches statues of dogs are placed at the feet of well-known people, including women and children, as symbols of loyalty and faith. In medieval art, such as Jan van Eyck's well-known "The Arnolfini Wedding" (1434), it has the same attribute of fidelity personified. From earliest times, however, there have been beautiful depictions of dogs—from ancient cave paintings and etchings such as the hunting scene with dogs in the Sahara Mountains dated at c. 3700 BCE to the dogs of ancient Egypt often represented as statues, such as the statuette of Anubis who represented the afterlife. This latter depiction is just one example of the dog being perceived as not only a faithful companion to the living, but a guide in the realm of the dead. In that regard it is interesting that recent research into numerous people's near-death experiences quote them as describing scenes of encountering animals traveling with them as they moved forward towards the light or as seeing their pets seeming to wait for them, the ones they had loved while on earth. Many hospice workers tell of their clients speaking of seeing their dogs in the circle of dead friends and relatives who are awaiting them as the dying person prepares to join them.

All of these traditions of spiritual guides, human and animal, can be equated with the name psychopomp, a guide who helps people through various transitions in life as well as an escort of souls to the afterlife. This term originates from the Greek words *pompos* (conductor or guide) and *psyche* (breath, life, mind, or soul). Like many shamans throughout history, ancient Celtic druids and druidesses in particular knew from first-hand experience of the mystical connection between humans and animals, and how animals guided not only the spiritual leaders of the tribes, but also ordinary people through life's conflicts and difficulties, sometimes helping them attain a new direction in life, a new identity. Celtic legends of their heroes had much in common with those found in other lands where the hero is led by animals to new geographical sites and new awarenesses. In numerous instances, helping animals not only enable a person to be transformed, but in a direct way they become his or her "double," an alter ego, another self waiting to be born. Red was that companion for me. In retrospect, she was a psychopomp who helped me move into a new direction, a new phase of my life.

At a time when I was struggling to discern what was bothering me so much our walks helped me begin to realize how unhappy I was in what I was doing with my life. I had read about "midlife," a time or period of uncertainty many people go through as they mature, when all the old ways don't seem to fulfill us anymore and we look for what our life is calling us to do; what perhaps we have ignored or been afraid to follow. For me, my growing unhappiness had to do with my highly active life, teaching, administering various programs at the college and nationally, and really wanting to spend more time in solitude, writing.

I had always loved books. My mother introduced me to them. She was my first teacher, the one who would sit me on her lap and read to me as a child, opening a much wider world for me than the series of little North Dakota towns we lived in. Once I started school, I was intrigued even more with the knowledge books and teachers taught me, the excitement of discovery, the elation of adventure. I would take my bike and pedal to the library in town and fill the basket on it with books I brought home to read. Even the librarian, a kind older lady with gray hair and always smiling, said she was amazed by my great variety of reading interests—and my thirst to learn. As a result of my reading, I did well academically in school, through grade school, high school, and college. It was natural, once finishing those years, that I wanted to study more as a doctoral student at the University of Notre Dame in South Bend, Indiana.

Reading books and loving them had its effect on my wanting to write them. I remember during my freshman year in high school, my English teacher had taken me under his wing, encouraging me to write. He mentored me, helping me revise a story I had written for his English class and then get it published. Seeing it in print with my name following the title affirmed that early desire and thirst to write more. My first book, really, was my doctoral thesis at Notre Dame which gave me great pleasure: first of all, of course, was the pleasure of actually finishing it, especially after having to make revisions one irksome professor demanded when it had been typed out in its entirety (which, as JoAnne reminded me, cost us a new washer and dryer!); secondly, seeing it finally in print gave me great pleasure. When it was published in book form, I would go into the local Catholic bookstore to stare at it among the numerous other books, so proud I had made it to a shelf, and, although only one book, I imagined adding more of my own. (Years later, in that same bookstore, I had an entire section of books under my name—a dream come true.)

But that was later. When I was hired at the College of St. Catherine, just out of graduate school, I took on a job description that was divided between teaching half-time and administering the pastoral ministry certificate program half-time. The so-called "half-time" changed dramatically, however, as more students joined the program. Not only was I advising them about what courses to take and helping them set up pastoral internship. I then also would have to search for qualified supervisors and train them. Within a few years, as coordinator of that program, I had ninety students in it. Yes, I was spending much more than "half time" on that job. Within a few more years, I went on to accept being chairperson of the burgeoning masters theology program with its new spirituality concentration. Because one of my two minors at Notre Dame had been in Christian spirituality, I was responsible for developing and teaching most of those initial courses in spirituality. From there, on my own initiative, I got the department's support in getting a new spirituality center, Wisdom Ways, co-sponsored by the college and the Sisters of St. Joseph of Carondelet, off the ground. Then I was elected national chairperson of NALM, and all that entailed, including being on a national committee, sponsored by the National Conference of Catholic Bishops, preparing for Pope John Paul II's meeting with the laity in San Francisco. The latter responsibility included, after the committee's input, my writing the talk that was given to the Pope in the Cathedral by a local layman. Needless to say, time for writing anything but monthly newsletters for NALM and articles for my own academic advancement at the college became very difficult. And let's not forget the addition to JoAnne's and my life of young sons.

All of these responsibilities, despite the stress, brought great satisfaction and happiness. But the hunger to write persisted as I grew frustrated with meetings, meetings, meetings. This frustration, of course, had its effect on my family as both JoAnne and I tried to balance two highly intense full-time careers while spending quality time with our sons. (JoAnne, of course, got stuck with most of the domestic chores, since I was gone so much, *and* since I obtusely thought I was always doing more around our home than my father ever did!)

As I became increasingly unhappy with my life, Red was my companion through this field of growing dissatisfaction, helping me to realize that I wanted something more; that I wanted to be a writer, and that I needed somehow to make a change so that I could. My walks with her almost every day helped me clarify this realization over time. One walk with her, in particular, became especially significant.

I remember it was a fall day, the ground covered with brightly-colored leaves, and Red and I were walking near the river, not far down the street from where the black dog had attacked us a few years before. Red was leading, as usual, following her nose, sniffing here and there until she discovered a new path we had not been on before. I recognized this, that we were headed in a new direction, but thought to myself, "Why not? She seems to know where she wants to go." A little while later, she headed up, off the beaten path, to a bluff overlooking the Mississippi River, with a fine view across the water to the other side. Reaching the top, I stopped her from walking further so as to enjoy the view.

It was then that I noticed, across the water from us, a whirlwind that was forming, twisting and turning, and scattering leaves into the air as it came toward us. I was amazed, taken in by the sight, and, yes, frightened, not knowing what to do! Was this a small hurricane; were we safe as it approached ever closer? Then in the sky above us, halfway between the bluff Red and I stood on and the distant shore across the river, I observed two white doves, their wings flapping in the wind, attempting, it seemed to maintain their balance. Moments passed as the forceful wind blew the fall leaves in ever-wider circles over the water, and as the doves continued flapping their wings. I glanced down to see where Red was, and saw that her fur was also being swept by the wind as I tried to maintain my own balance. She too was looking up in the sky, at the wind and the doves.

Then, suddenly, everything changed—the wind stopped, the water calmed, and the doves disappeared. Silence. Across the water I saw the sun appear, its bright rays, hidden by the force of the wind and the swirling leaves, shining, lighting up the horizon. I paused with Red at my feet, herself quiet and unmoving, looking off in the direction of the river. Standing there in silence for a moment, trying to take in what had just happened, I then led her down the bluff, bewildered as I was, it seemed, not knowing what we'd seen, but aware of it being a pivotal moment of some kind. Months later, while taking courses at the Jung Institute in Zurich, Switzerland, I had a session with the Jungian therapist Ian Baker, and described the experience to him. I had not told anyone about what seemed to be such an unusual occurrence, like a vision of sorts that I had with Red by my side. Ian, with his extensive knowledge of symbols, was able to help me begin to clarify its possible meaning.

In a lot of spiritual traditions, doves, usually white in color, symbolize love or peace, or often are seen as messengers from the divine or the spiritual realm. In Hebrew Scriptures, in the story of Noah and the Flood (Gen 6-9), a dove is released by Noah from the ark after the flood in order to find land; it comes back carrying a freshly plucked olive leaf, a sign that the flood was receding. After several more times being sent out by Noah, it finally does not return to the ark, a sure sign that it was now safe for Noah, his family, and the animals in the ark to leave it. Later, a rainbow is sent as a symbol of the new covenant God makes with humankind that "the waters will never again become a flood to destroy all things of flesh" (Gen 9:12–17). This story, then, with its dove and the rainbow is a sign of hope of new life, of a new relationship with God, and of new beginnings.

In later Jewish writings, the Talmud, the body of Jewish legend and law, compares the spirit of God to a dove that hovers over the face of the waters, and in writings associated with the Jewish Kabbalah, especially those of Vilna Gaon, an 18th century mystic, a dove symbolizes the human soul.

As the Jews saw the dove as representative of the spirit of God, in Christian iconography, the dove represents the Holy Spirit, the third person of the Blessed Trinity, vividly expressed in the story of the Holy Spirit descending on Jesus in the form of a dove after his baptism, affirming, along with the voice of God from the sky that "This is my Son, the Beloved; my favor rests on him" (Matt 3:16–17).

So, in terms of my experience with Red on the bluff overlooking the Mississippi river that day, it could be associated with an invitation to consider something new in my life, a call to my soul and deeper self. And, along with Ian, I was especially drawn to what the Talmud said, comparing the white dove to the spirit of God "hovering over the face of the waters." That was exactly what I saw and where I saw it. The Christian view also identifies the dove with the Spirit of God affirming God's son as "beloved." Again, I remembered what the spiritual writer, Henri Nouwen, wrote in *Life of the Beloved*, a book I had used for various classes, that "we are all the beloved sons and daughters of God, called to live a life based upon that knowledge." If I was to pay attention to my experience, it seemed that I should affirm the call of God's spirit to embrace a new direction in my life—a message given in a somewhat dramatic way, initiated by Red's leading me there, to the bluff; in effect becoming my spirit guide, my psychopomp.

But my vision had two doves!! "What is the meaning of two?" I asked Ian. He explained to me how humanity from earliest times seems to have had a fascination with numerals, associating them with different spiritual meanings. Two often represents peace and harmony, and for the Chinese the symbol yin and yang combined, without separation, brings together masculine and feminine energies, darkness and light. In China, two is an auspicious number because Chinese people believe that "good comes in pairs." Two is a symbol of wholeness; two unites and brings an end to separateness; its energy is that of the Sacred Feminine or Great Mother. Two comes to us as a reminder to be true to ourselves; two beckons us to choose. Two suggests that one is at a point in life where one is looking for some sense of balance; it means to have faith and to keep trusting; it can lead to new harmony. Usually two also has the meaning of a double, of being twinned. Twins appear often in the guise of animals and birds, and are recognized as a beneficial sign. When they appear in dreams and fairy tales, they represent, Ian said, an invitation to surrender, to find new expressions of creativity.

Well, needless to say, when I told Ian of my unhappiness with my life and my desire to write, he strongly suggested and affirmed that I follow the various levels of meaning found in my experience with Red on the bluff. He also volunteered that he and I could stay in touch with emails, since calling between St. Paul, Minnesota, and Zurich, Switzerland would be so expensive. (This was before skyping or Facebook video-calls had been invented.) So my conversations with Ian continued, after my return from Zurich, as I attempted to discern what I should do about my dilemma, my increasing unhappiness and search for a new direction.

Some months later, another strange event happened to me with Red as my guide. Jung would have called it "synchronicity," a term describing an event or events, seemingly unrelated or un-caused, that come together in meaningful ways for the benefit of the recipient or recipients. As Jung expressed it, "meaningful coincidences occur with apparently no causal relationship yet seem to be meaningfully related."

Regarding my experience of synchronicity, I had just returned from teaching and as I opened the front door and entered the hallway of our home, I saw Red sleeping at the top of the steps, a favorite place. Closing the door, however, with her now awake,

I became aware of what seemed to be a powerful stream of light, coming down the steps from her spot, seeming to invite me to go up and follow its origin. Now, obviously, the steps had been lit with light before, but this time the light seemed especially powerful, again, like a vision, pulling me upward. I was very conscious that this was not ordinary light. Somewhat bewildered, I kept going up the steps to the second floor where Red was now standing, and on into my study where the light seemed to be leading me.

Entering my study, with Red now at my side, I saw the powerful beam of light, focused, it seemed, on an icon of the desert father, John Cassian. Some years before, I had commissioned a friend to write this icon, and had asked him to paint on the book which the saint is holding a favorite saying, "The bond between friends cannot be broken." Instead, he had printed another saying which, at the time I saw it when it arrived in the mail, disappointed me. But now, in my study the beam of light was focused directly on the words of Cassian that had been written on the icon, "Let us pass from what is visible to the life of the inner man." I stopped and stared at what I saw, attempting to take in a new awareness that I believed I should follow: the awareness, along with my earlier experience on the bluff, that I needed to pay closer attention to my inner life that was telling me of my strong desire to become a writer.

In my next email to Ian, I shared with him that vision of light. I told him that I realized on one level that the light was bright sunlight coming through the window of my study that afternoon, focused "coincidentally" on the icon. But on another, deeper level, it was a light that had, along with Red, invited me to follow it up to my study where my computer with its word-processor sat on a table near my desk. The intensity of light, the focus of it on Cassian's powerful words, I took to have great significance. But again, what to do with that? That was the question. And Red, my psychopomp, had been there with me, encouraging me with her presence to follow the light and pay attention to it, and especially to the message of the icon illuminated by it.

Sometime later after this experience with the light, in preparation for my teaching about the Celtic saints who had interested
me for years, I came across the story of a Saint Cuthbert, whom I
had never heard of before. The Venerable Bede, the eighth-century
English monk, now known as "the Father of English history," had
written about him, and although Bede had written many stories
about other Celtic saints, I could tell Cuthbert was a special favorite of his, a saint considered to be Northern England's most
popular saint and one of Christianity's greatest spiritual guides.

As I got into my reading Bede's account of Cuthbert's life I
found myself identifying closely with this monk who was constantly torn between the active life and the contemplative. According
to Bede, Cuthbert at an early age, probably about seventeen years
old, had joined the Celtic monastery at Melrose, Scotland, begun
by St. Aidan, an Irish monk. Evidently Cuthbert was very talented
and recognized for his leadership, for he served as a guestmaster at
another monastery, Ripon, then was elected prior at Melrose and
then at another monastery, Lindisfarne, located on a holy isle off
the coast of northern England. There, inundated with administrative responsibilities for years, he finally chose to give those up and
move to a smaller island, Inner Farne Island, where he attempted
to live as a solitaire. Building a cell in which to live, he settled into
his own soul-making, living simply in prayer and fasting—until
great numbers of people sought him out as a spiritual guide. He
loved his island and his new lifestyle, despite so many interrup-
tions, and lived there for about ten years—until again his life was
interrupted by the English king himself sailing to the island and
begging him to become bishop of Lindisfarne. Surely unhappy at
the request, considering the number of duties associated with such
a position, he still agreed to assume a very active ministry once
more. Three years later, however, deciding that he needed to return
to a more solitary life, he resigned as bishop and returned to his
hermitage on his beloved Inner Farne where he died.

After reading this story of St. Cuthbert, it was as if a light
went on in my head. Here was a man, devoted to his calling, an
administrator and a spiritual guide, who chose at a certain point

in his life to resign his duties as a prior and go in search of solitude; a solitude that was never perfect, but one that allowed him greater freedom to be available to people as well as having more time for prayer. In effect, Cuthbert's story became profoundly revelatory for me; it touched my soul, for it provided me with an example that I too could follow. It showed me that I too could make a transition from the many duties I now held; I too could request, as Cuthbert had done, resigning from the various programs I administered and go to full-time teaching which would allow me, I hoped, more time to write.

Bede's story of Cuthbert helped me realize my possibilities, seated, as I was, in the big green leather chair in my study, with Red, as usual, by my side. First led by her to the bluff overlooking the river, a body of water often associated with liminality and the opening of doors; then to the profound vision of light, often equated with revelation, and the words of Cassian reminding me of what I must attend to; and finally discovering a story that offered an alternative to my work—all with Reddy, my spirit guide.

I wrote Ian about my latest revelation, and my determination now to change what could be changed. I told him how I intended to go to the chair of the theology department and request that we find someone else to do the administrative part of my responsibilities, so that I could go to full-time teaching, and pursue the call to be a writer too.

THREE

Good Friday

Time passes quickly, it seems, as we age. The years following my decision to retire from administrative duties and teach full-time sped by. It wasn't easy writing, I discovered, when I was constantly preparing classes, reading papers and tests, but the research I did for the various books I began to write helped me with my teaching, and the students in my courses with their questions and comments contributed to my writing books. Red was always there at my side—not seated next to me in our chair, but lying on the floor at my feet where I wrote at my computer ten books and numerous articles. She continued to be a constant presence of support and encouragement, patiently lying there, waiting for me to take a break to let her out or to take her for our walk.

Before JoAnne and I knew it, our sons had grown up, and were working and living outside the home. One day, as the two of us were seated in the living-room, we started talking about the changes in our lives, and how quickly John and Dan had grown from babies into young men. "I can't believe it," I said with tears in my eyes. "First they're babies in the stroller, and suddenly they have their own cars!" With the boys gone, the two of us were facing another transition. It would be a major change. We had decided to sell our home. I was to move into a smaller house not far from the Minnesota State Fairgrounds while JoAnne would stay in our old home until it was sold. This change in our lives, of course, was a major change for Red too as she moved with me while our Princeton home was on the market.

With all the commotion and disruption in our own lives, I failed to fully recognize the effect this would have on Red. It was not like one could sit down and explain it to her, but it became clear the first morning after she and I had moved into the new house on Asbury Street. As I went to leave for school, I heard behind me as I closed the door, a long, sad howl. She was alone in this strange house in a strange neighborhood, and didn't know what was going on!! Her howl, of course, stopped me in my tracks, and I didn't know what to do. I had to go to class, and she had to stay there, in this strange house. All I could do was yell through the door, "It's okay, Reddy." And trying to further reassure her, I said, "I won't be long." I had never heard such a mournful sound before, coming from my beloved dog.

We both had adjusting to do! Over time, we got used to the new arrangement, offering, I think in many ways, comfort to each other. That lasted for a month or two, before the emerging routine of my going to and from class-with Red waiting for me was interrupted. I had made a decision to tear down the rickety deck, attached to the house in back, and replace it with a three-season porch. While that was being done, with workmen coming in and out, I decided Red needed to go back to our old home, away from all the din. So Red returned to Princeton, to another house which was empty much of the day, as JoAnne continued at her work and Dan was living with his friend, Mark, in Roseville. John was on his own in an apartment in St. Paul after his first year in law school. I missed Red tremendously, but knew it was for only a short time, I thought. Well, of course it took much longer than the workmen had promised—as these projects always do.

One afternoon, however, I got a frantic call from Dan that Red was missing. She had evidently gotten out of the backyard on Princeton when someone had left the back gate open, and she had disappeared. Dan said he was going to look for her, and I told him I'd be right over to help him. We were desperate, afraid that she'd be kidnapped or run over by a car. While Dan searched on foot, I drove up and down the neighborhood, with the windows down, yelling her name. Finally, Dan found her on the next block, in the alley, close to the route we used to take, leading to the river. She seemed to be happy, Dan said, and relieved to be found. But she was never on her own before, except for once when workmen had left the gate open and she was gone for a short time, alarming us then as well. Now, I thought, she might have been looking for me, since I was no longer living on Princeton, and she didn't know where I'd gone. On a mission to find me? Or just curious, her "nose-i-ness" taking over once again with the opportunity of freedom! Frustrated, angry, afraid, Dan spanked her hard, while I watched helplessly. She didn't know any better, I thought, but both Dan and I had been terrified that something had happened to her. Again, she never fought back, or growled, but accepted her "punishment" with patience and endurance—as she always did.

Finally, when the new porch was done in mid-November, Reddy and I were reunited again. She seemed to adjust better now to her new environment—as I did as well. Our walks together in the neighborhood gave us both the chance to explore new territory and eventually develop our own routes. Inside the house, I began buying some new furniture. Along with the older furniture that was brought from our house on Princeton Avenue, I placed a new chair in the living-room. This Victorian-style chair with its carved wood and fine-colored material I wanted to protect. I told Red to stay off of it, saying, "No!" when she first jumped up on it. She looked at me, recognizing my tone of voice, as I placed her on the floor again. Later, however, I found her happily settled on it, again, as if on a special throne for herself alone. I told her once again to get down, and picked her up and put her on the old couch. Within no time, she was back on the chair. Red had that stubborn streak in her, and she knew what she liked! (And, as I mentioned earlier, she never really did listen to me, anyway!) I finally gave up trying to change her determination to be comfortable there. She did look like a princess, I thought, after her haircut, sitting there majestically and very self-satisfied, enjoying her spot, wagging her tail when I walked by, as if to say, "guess who won that one!"

Red and I were alone in the new house on Christmas since we hadn't sold the old one yet. But we still got together on Christmas eve for our usual dinner on Princeton Avenue with JoAnne's family, our sons, and the opening of gifts. Red was in her element, obviously happy to be at a party where others like herself were having a good time.

It was that winter, however, that I first began to notice changes in Red. Was she getting a little deaf and having some difficulty in seeing? I didn't think so, initially; I mean, she seemed to hear *anything* or *anyone* in our new neighborhood that I did not. Of course in response to what she heard, she would bark loudly, warning me of potential dangers. (Such a sweetheart!) But there had been the time that fall, after she and I had moved in, that I experienced the poignant moment of me coming home through the back door rather than coming in the front, and my seeing her waiting for me at the front door, her back toward me, her tail wagging happily, evidently in anticipation of my entrance there. I called to her, since she still hadn't heard me come in. She turned, then, and saw me at last, and came running, overjoyed to see me. Now that was so endearing, her initial anticipation waiting for me, and then her joy when she finally saw me; so affirming of her love for me. I was surprised, however, that she hadn't heard nor seen me initially.

And then there was her changing appearance. After the holidays, when the housing market in the Twin Cities had fallen through and it was increasingly difficult to sell our house on Princeton, it slowly dawned on me that there was something different about Red—her red hair was graying, and she looked much thinner. Then I became extremely alarmed when I noticed one day that I could see the vertebrae in her back! Still other warning signs appeared that I could no longer ignore: her struggles to defecate; her bloody stools. Seeing her slow movement up the stairs, I said to myself, "that's not right," still hoping that it was temporary, just a sign of aging—not of her demise! But this was the dog who always bounded up and down the steps, especially in the morning, starting our day. It finally dawned on me, "Oh, my God, she needs help!" I decided to take her to the animal clinic in Eagan where she had been going for years and have the veterinarian Dr. Karen Wheeler examine her. Any visit to the vet, however, was always a traumatic experience for Red. She would huddle under the chair or bench in the office, shivering violently, as we waited for Dr. Wheeler or one of her assistants to appear for Red's exams. I would try to coax her out, to hold her on my lap, to calm her fears, but she was obviously petrified. Sometimes I would just pull on the leash until she was forced to come out, and then pick her up and hold her close, trying to get her to stop shaking. But she never growled at Dr. Wheeler when she arrived, or resisted her touch. Red certainly had reasons for her fears, since so many earlier visits had resulted in pain: when she was spayed as a puppy, for example, or, as an older dog, when she had her gums cleaned and even one or two teeth removed in surgery. But she did not take it out on others; she always maintained a friendly demeanor, something that Dr. Wheeler mentioned more than once—how gentle Red was, and friendly.

This time, as usual, after arriving and sitting in one of the offices waiting for Dr. Wheeler to appear, Red crouched under the bench on which I was sitting, and trembled as she often did. I picked her up and held her in my arms, trying to ease her fear, but this time she seemed to tremble even more than previous visits! Tests, ultra-sound, urinalysis, blood tests, followed Dr. Wheeler's physical exam of her. Unfortunately the tests Red underwent that day did not show what was the cause of her problems, and so all Dr. Wheeler could do was give her antibiotics, put her on steroids, and suggest that I keep her well-fed while watching for any signs of something unusual occurring. This was going to become a common theme in the months ahead: despite thousands of dollars spent on tests—ultrasound, heart, kidneys, liver—no one would be able to tell us what was wrong with Red. "The good news is that it's not the liver; it's not the kidneys," Dr. Wheeler said that day, and then the refrain I would hear often: "The bad news: we don't know what it is."

So we went home together, Red and I, and continued our
routine once classes had begun again after the January term had
ended: I going back and forth to St. Kates, and she waiting patiently for me to return—always happy, ecstatic when I opened the
door. But she didn't seem to be getting any better, even with the
medication she had been given initially. By February 6, Dr. Wheeler suggested that I take her to the University of Minnesota Animal
Hospital in hopes that the staff there might diagnose the problem.
Increasingly anxious about my dear dog, I called for an appoint-
ment. Two days later I took Red in to be dropped off at 9:15 in the
morning for a series of tests they were going to give her that day.

We drove up to the modern facility where new arrivals
would be admitted. I had never been on the grounds before nor
inside this building. What hit me was that, unlike so many other
hospitals I'd visited in my life, *this one* was serving animals exclu-
sively. After checking in at the main desk, I waited in the lobby,
with Red, of course, cowering in fear under my chair. I offered
words of comfort, and picked her up and held her. Then, after
what seemed to be a very long time, a male orderly, tall, burly,
dressed in white, came to take her away for the tests. He seemed
nonchalant, like it was no big deal, but I will never forget the look
in Red's eyes as this total stranger led her away on the leash. She
literally stopped and turned around and looked at me with the
saddest eyes that seemed to ask, "What's going on here? Where
is he taking me?" And even more difficult for me to see, "Why
aren't you coming with?" I spoke to her then, assuring her I'd be
back for her soon. She turned around then and patiently allowed
the total stranger to take her away. I left the hospital in tears,
wondering what was happening to the dog I'd loved since she was
a little puppy, and anguishing at my inability, my powerlessness
to prevent her from experiencing any more pain.

My day did not go well. I felt so helpless, and was so worried at what was happening to her! I went to my first class that
morning, an introductory theology course for undergraduates,
and started it by telling them that I was quite upset after leaving
my beloved dog at the animal hospital and not knowing what was

happening to her. I choked up in relating this, and a silence settled over the classroom until some of these young students, moved by compassion, began hesitantly offering me comfort. Later that day, when I picked Red up at the hospital, the doctor's assistant commented on what a sweetheart Red had been, patiently lying on her side and stomach as she was probed and examined. But the tests on her had been inconclusive and they still did not know what she had. All they could do was assign me tylosin capsules and other tablets, and a certain type of dogfood that would give her more strength. I picked up all of it at the pharmacy and drove Red home. She seemed relieved to be reunited with me, and back to the warmth and security of our house. Unfortunately, though, for her I was told that she must not have any more human food. So began a pattern: she would sit there, by my chair, as I ate, waiting for her "share"; I would tell her, "I can't give this to you anymore—for your own sake. 'No other food except that prescribed,' the vet told me." Red was not amused! And for her to accept and eat some of the "horse-pills" I had to give her, I wrapped them in the dog-food she was required to eat—only to have her take them in her mouth and then spit them out—to my chagrin. Oh she was a smart dog!

Less than two weeks later, on February 21, Lent began with the Ash Wednesday service reminding us Catholics, with the smudging of ashes on our foreheads, of our own mortality, "Remember that you are dust, and to dust you will return." Ashes, in this tradition, symbolize our need for penance, and for repentance; they also symbolize grief. At the time, I did not know how much *this Lent* would be a period of increasing suffering for Reddy, and of intense grief for me, culminating with her death on Good Friday, forty-four days after I received the ashes on my forehead.

As the Lenten days unfolded with my feeding Red special meals and watching her closely, I began to realize what a total lack of awareness I had that dogs' lives are limited. I hadn't had a dog since Spotty when I was in grade school, and, until now, I had never really thought about Red's aging. Not really! To me she was always the puppy I had brought home who had grown into such a beautiful creature, affectionate, loving, adding happiness to my life on the good days and comfort on the bad. Now she was sick with something nobody was able to diagnose! That's when I started reading about how long a dog Red's breed and size was expected to live! American cocker spaniels, I discovered, could be expected to live from twelve to fifteen years. Red, I thought, was only eleven! Surely what she was facing now couldn't be fatal! There had to be a cure! Hope sustained me at this time of her "rehabilitation" on steroids and special dog food; hope and the small unspoken "comfort," knowing, I thought, that at least she has no sense of mortality; that if this was a fatal illness, she at least wouldn't have to worry. I could do that for both of us!

Weeks passed. As I visited the pharmacy at the university hospital to get more special food for Red, I began to notice on the faces of others their concern when they brought their sick animals in. I also saw on one or two occasions families coming out, without their pet, in tears and anguish. I remember one young family in particular, two parents holding the hands of their small children who were in tears, and their trying to comfort them. What can one say in these situations? "She's in heaven now, and will look down on us with love." Or, "We will always remember him." Or, "We will find another pet." Or, "It's okay to cry." Or, "She's with God, and God will take care of her."

The canned food seemed to give Red a bit of added energy, although Red's groomer, Carol, when she heard how much it was costing me, suggested that I just give Red a diet of lean fried hamburger and rice. "That will be fine; it's always worked for my dogs." So I began to intermix the canned food with Carol's recommended meals. What I found endearing about Red was how she would first wait for the hamburger, the human food, and gobble that down before moving on to the canned dog food. She always was highly discriminating in her preferences—even up to her last days!

As my fear for Red only increased that first month of Lent, I reached out to JoAnne and my close friends, talking with them about our dog and my terror at losing her. This not knowing what was adversely affecting her was making me feel crazy. All the tests were not providing a diagnosis and thus no prognosis! It reminded me of the time when I received a call after an evening class from JoAnne that our son Dan had just been taken to the hospital in an ambulance. I was terrified, and immediately drove to the hospital, parked my car, and ran in. I was directed to the room where JoAnne was seated next the bed where Dan lay, with doctors examining him. He was perspiring heavily, highly agitated, but conscious. Tests were given, and we waited to be told what was causing his distress. The results were inconclusive—they didn't know what was happening. (I had always thought doctors would!) JoAnne went home, obviously anxious, and I stayed with Dan in the room. At one point, he turned his face toward me, and asked, "Dad, am I going to die?" What could I say, except, with the conviction of a loving parent whose sons mean everything, "No, we will find out what's going on! You are not going to die!" The next day, after more tests, including an MRI, there was still no diagnosis, which I discovered happened more frequently than people are aware; sometimes the cause of an illness cannot be found. Such was the case for Dan and us, with antibiotics given and his eventual discharge, after some days in the hospital, with them telling us it might be a rare form of mononucleosis (mono). All JoAnne and I could do was be there for him, reassuring him that he was going to be alright.

So also now with Red. Nobody seemed to know what the cause of her illness was, nor even what the illness itself was—other than seeing the physical results of her increasing loss of weight and on occasions having blood in her stools.

I couldn't imagine losing her, or what my life would be like without her! Now in my new house, she was the one who made my life tolerable, who eased my loneliness and stress with her constant and unconditional love. My friend, Mary Kaye, told me that for men, especially, dogs mean so much. "I only saw my father cry once, and it was when his dog died. He wouldn't talk about the loss, but would sit out on the porch or somewhere else in the house alone, and I could see his tears."

Life went on, one day at a time, with Red seeming to get weaker, and me more anxious. She, however had not lost her appetite, especially liking the "new" diet Carol had advised with the canned dogfood. One evening, as I fried the hamburger, she was at my feet, eagerly watching me prepare supper. As I moved around the kitchen, in a hurry to move the hamburger and rice to her dish, I almost stepped on her. In anger, and frustration, I said to her impatiently, "For God's sake, Red, get a life!" She, of course, shied away, looking as if she didn't understand my shortness and tone of voice. Then I realized what I had said—and that that was exactly what she was now trying to do: to somehow overcome the unknown disease that seemed to be destroying her. "Get a life!" Oh, God, I felt so guilty and ashamed, and picked her up, petted her, and told her, "That's alright, Reddy, you are a good dog, and you deserve a good meal." I held her in my arms, and cried, so afraid of losing her.

The good news, if there was any at this time, was that after years spent consigned to her kennel at night (and every night reluctantly going into it), at least now I put her in my bed where she slept happily at my feet. She loved that, it seemed, bounding up the steps—when she could—and settling in. When she couldn't get up in the bed on her own I'd lift her in my arms and place her there. She seemed content, luxuriating in the blankets.

As St. Patrick's Day approached, I prepared for a trip I had planned months before, just to get out of Minnesota for a while after another long winter. JoAnne was busy with the legislative session. I had no knowledge at the time I made the plans, however, that Red would be in the condition she was now in. I was to fly to Hawaii for a short vacation during spring break at the college, and stay with a friend whom I had known for years, now living on the island of Maui. Dan had agreed to stay at my place while I was away taking care of Red which I highly appreciated, but I still felt horrible that I was leaving her when she seemed so sick. But off I went on St. Patrick's Day itself, anxious for her, but happy to be leaving Minnesota. Maui, of course, was wonderful with its warm climate and beautiful scenic coast. I enjoyed the travel around it, including the Road to Hana, swimming in the ocean, and not to mention the great seafood meals. After five days of this bliss, however, as I was preparing to board the plane for my trip back, I received a frantic call from Dan on my cellphone. I knew this was not going to be good news! "I am at an emergency clinic," he told me with strain in his voice. "Red had bloody, ketchup-like diarrhea tonight, and I didn't know what to do so I brought her here! When are you coming home?"

"Oh, God," I said, "I am at the airport right now, and my plane leaves in an hour. I will be back in the morning your time."

"Well," he said, obviously not pleased, "hurry." He had taken her in around 11:45 that night, and after more tests she had been discharged at 12:35 a.m.

Needless to say, the flight back was not pleasant, seeming to take forever. Returning to Minnesota from Hawaii is never pleasant, but all during this flight I was filled with anxiety, thinking about Red and praying for her, not knowing what to expect upon landing. When I arrived home Dan and Red met me at the door, Dan explaining this latest crisis and Red feebly wagging her tail, happy to see me. She seemed weak, although the bleeding had stopped, but obviously with less energy than when I had left five days before. I spent the weekend going through the usual re-entry process—paying bills, reading student papers, preparing for the last couple months of class before the semester ended—and watching Red.

The week after my return, while continuing to worry about Red, I was back in the classroom, mornings, afternoons, and Friday night for a Weekend College course, plus being involved in meetings with students and colleagues. In the midst of this schedule, I was observing how difficult it now was for her to climb the steps from the family room in the basement to the kitchen, struggling to get up each of the steps, going so slowly and deliberately when she used to bound up without hesitation. Then the time I took her out for a walk that week only to discover she couldn't go more than half a block from the house before she had to stop, unable to go any further. I had to pick her up, and carry her home. That was so hard to see, and I was in tears when we got back. And then too her bowel movements continued now to be filled with blood. One time, as I walked into the kitchen and saw blood on the floor, she looked so ashamed of herself! I told her, "Reddy, it's okay, you couldn't help it; it's alright; you're a good dog." Then remembering, of course, that I had been the one when she was a puppy to encourage shame as a way of preventing any messes in the house.

The next week was the beginning of Holy Week, in the Christian calendar the week we remember as the last week of Jesus's passion and death. In addition to classes the first three days of that week, I had a men's spirituality breakfast and discussion Wednesday morning at 7:15 at Wisdom Ways which I had to facilitate. The good news was that after it was over I had the rest of the week without responsibilities so I would be able to stay home with Red. That was the week, however, when she took a turn for the worse, the beginning of her own agony and death.

Wednesday, April 4, she would not come out of her kennel in the morning. I had placed it next to my bed, due to her sickness and bleeding. This was so unlike her when she was well, eager to begin the new day with excitement and happiness as I opened the kennel door. This time she didn't move, just lay there, barely looking up at me when I called her name. Not knowing what to expect, I wondered if she'd bite me or experience a change of personality in her pain—but, no, she lifted her head with patient endurance, remaining true to her usual loving self. I reached in, grabbed her front legs, and pulled her gently toward me. I thought then of my mother's friend, Donna Kipp, who when she was dying did not want to have visitors to her hospital room. I was told that people preparing to die often withdraw from human contact, and genuinely want solitude. Was Red preparing to die, or just too weak to move from her kennel? Or both. I didn't know.

After facilitating the men's group that morning, I stayed with Red the rest of the day, holding her at times, and trying to offer her some comfort. I could tell, however, that she was weak and not all that responsive. And, whenever I left her sight, she would look around for me, needing, it seemed, reassurance that I was there for her. She seemed especially anxious. I put her beside me on the couch, like the days in our old house when she snuggled next to me and slept. That night, before I put her in her kennel, I kissed her on her beautiful forehead, and told her, "Reddy, I love you; I always will."

Holy Thursday, the day remembered for Jesus's last supper with his disciples, I awoke anxious and afraid, hearing nothing from her kennel. I was terrified that she must have died during the night, only to discover her huddled by the toilet, perhaps seeking comfort from the cool floor. When I helped her up, she drank a lot of water, evidently severely dehydrated. I knew I had to do something then; she needed help. So I put her in the car and we drove back to the university animal hospital, hoping there was something they could do. Again, once again, Red was taken from me for more tests. I don't know how long I sat in the waiting-room until Dr. Diana Saam came out and took me to her office to share the results with me. She began by telling me that Red was found to have significant blood loss anemia, and probably needed a blood transfusion if she was to survive. She recommended that I consider the procedure the next day if there was no improvement. Tears welled up, as I heard her talk, realizing that she's telling me Red may not make it, and asking myself, "So is this it? Is this the end of hope? Oh, my God, I don't want Red to die!" Dr. Saam must have seen the look of trepidation on my face, for she tried to comfort me. (Mark Doty, the author of *Dog Years: A Memoir*, refers to the fact that a veterinarian has *two* patients to care for: the sick or dying animal, and its owner; both are suffering. Dr. Saam would have three, Red, myself, and my son, Dan.)

I called Dan after returning home with Red, and asked him to come over and have supper with me and the dog we had raised together since she was a little puppy. By this time, aware that this might be our last meal together with her, I told him over the phone, "I'm not sure she's going to make it." When he arrived, Dan had a look of anguish on his face, and expressed how worried he was. Red loved him dearly, as he did her. After our move to the new house, she would anticipate him coming over to visit. I would tell her, "Danny's coming," and she'd go to the door. I'd ask, "Where's Dan?" and she'd look for him around the house. Now so sick, she still wagged her tale when he came in.

We talked about what to do; what could be done? As we shared a meal of soup and sandwiches, this time Red did not beg for any morsel; too sick, she had stopped eating. Dan and I had shared many years together with her, and now we shared a deep sense of desperation, not knowing, hoping against hope that somehow she would revive. Hoping for a miracle. I called JoAnne, after Dan left, and told her about a possible blood transfusion for Red. "I've already spent thousands of dollars, and the transfusion would be at least two thousand more."

JoAnne thought a bit, always reflective before she spoke on major issues, and then said quietly, "I think you should have them do it. If that doesn't work, at least you'll know you did everything you could for her."

That night, before climbing into bed, I blessed Red three times, and signed a cross on her forehead three times, as she lay huddled in her kennel at the foot of my bed. It was a ritual I had used when my father was dying, and Mom and I spent the night which was to be his last in the hospital room after his stroke. This night, I prayed that Red would somehow survive. The night, how-ever, did not go well at all. I had barely fallen asleep when I heard her moan slightly for the first time—and begin to breathe heavily and frequently: signs I had been told to watch for. What should I do? I was panic-stricken, not knowing whether to wait out the night or get her to the emergency ward at the hospital? I decided I had to do something NOW—no matter what the cost. I did not want to see (or hear) her suffer!

Bundling her up in a blanket, I got her into the car and drove to the hospital. The orderly on duty took her from me, and I waited anxiously for what seemed hours. Finally I was seen by a Dr. Mil-lard, a young veterinarian who after seeing the results of the latest tests recommended that she be hospitalized immediately with a blood transfusion that morning. I thought about it; I wanted to do the right thing. But I preferred to take her home with me for the night, if it was to be her last. I told him this and he agreed, but suggested if I noticed an obvious increase in her pain or increased labor in breathing that I bring her back immediately. We set 8:00

a.m. as the time for her readmission. That would give me only a few hours of sleep (if I could get it) before returning, but I still wanted her to be with me at home.

Returning from the hospital, not knowing what to do, I laid Red on the bed with me, determined that if this was to be our last night together, she and I would both be comforted by my holding her. Again, I prayed for a miracle; I prayed to Saints Brigit and Francis, the two saints known for their friendship with animals, that my dear dog would be spared; that we could enjoy together two, three, four more years . . . "Please, God," I begged, "don't take her away now!" And remembering, as we lay there in these early morning hours, that today was Good Friday, I told Red: "We're going to fight this, Reddy; you and me. We're not going to give in; if we can get through this day, maybe we can beat it." Previous nights, when she had begun sleeping with me after we moved into the new house, she had always wanted her own space sleeping near the end of the bed, but this night, this last night, she didn't resist when I held her next to me, next to my heart. I fell asleep, exhausted.

That morning when I awoke, there obviously was no time for Red's and my usual routine. No, I hugged her and told her how much I loved her, and got her into the car and back to the university hospital where she was quickly readmitted. Oh, God, I felt so helpless, so bereft of hope, *yet still hoping* that the blood transfusion would help prolong her life for at least a few years more, perhaps. It wasn't long, however, although it seemed forever, before a doctor came out to tell me that in the preparation for the blood transfusion they had discovered that Red had cancer—and there was no cure for it. I couldn't believe it, that after months of expensive tests they hadn't been able to diagnose cancer earlier. Even I knew, in my own limited research, that the leading cause of death in both dogs and cats is cancer or kidney disease. I was angry and mostly scared, knowing now that there was nothing more that could be done, and that it was now necessary to euthanize Reddy in order to stop her suffering before it got worse.

I was intent that Red not die alone, with strangers. I remembered how the doctor, after the stroke that left my father brain-dead, had told us to leave his hospital room after our decision to turn off the respirator that kept oxygen flowing into his lungs. "Never," I said, "we will stay," and we did, holding onto his arms as he took his last breath. So with Reddy, animals, like people, I thought, should be surrounded by loved ones when it is time to pass over. I called Dan and told him he should come to the hospital as soon as he could, no later than noon. He had been expecting a call, but not with this devastating news. He arrived before noon, and we were shown into the office of Dr. Saam who told us we could use it for whatever time we needed.

When Red was brought in, she seemed fully conscious, quiet, happy to see us, with her tail wagging softly—but, I noticed, she also was licking her lips in anxiety. She was wearing a scarf, with Easter eggs and lilies on it, something that some sensitive orderly must have given her. After Dr. Saam left us to be alone with Red, we spent an hour taking turns holding her, telling her how much we loved her, telling her we would never forget her. She seemed to understand, and to relax, happy to be the recipient of all this attention, affirmation, and love. Observing Dan's holding her, I thought how in this office of such a compassionate veterinarian who gave us all the time we needed to tell Red goodbye, the full circle of life had come to Dan and me. He, my dear son, and I had started together in joy, seeing Red playing with her siblings, choosing her, and taking her home; and now, as we held her in our arms, talking to her, attempting to reassure her, we were together in our grief. Eleven years that had gone so quickly, yet filled with happiness, a happiness that she had brought us with her love.

When we knew that it was time, that we couldn't prolong this forever, I went out and found Dr. Saam. Then, while Dan and I held dear Reddy, she injected the needle. Red's body relaxed immediately and seemed to soften in our arms as her last breath escaped from her. She was still, but seemed not so much dead as sleeping. And, as I gazed down at her, memories of happier times came to me: her running through the fields of grass that first day we were taking her home; the joy and friendliness she manifest at greeting friends; our walks, especially the one in which she had led me to the bluff overlooking the river; her lying at my feet, stretched out, sleeping near my computer when I was writing book after book. I looked down at her now, and she seemed so overwhelmingly beautiful, relaxed, no longer suffering! It was a scene of total tranquility. And yet our spirits, Dan's and mine, rose up in grief, horrendous sadness, and indignation, witnessing her last breath. How could this be—that our beautiful dog, our friend, our companion was dead?! How could this be!! Our only consolation in that moment of desolation was knowing that she died in loving arms, happy, for the attention we gave her that last hour. She died surrounded by love, immersed in love—as she had given us so much unconditional love over the years. I told her to go with Mel who had played so often with her in the backyard on Princeton, throwing the ball which she loved to run and catch and bring back to him. And to go with my dad who loved her too. "They will take care of you, Reddy, until I come." And, then, as Dr. Saam left the room, giving us a little time to be alone with our sorrow, both Dan and I, son and father, burst into tears and held each other.

Reddy was gone, as was the roller-coaster ride we had been on, one of hope and fear and despair and hope again. Now it was grief that Dan and I would face, deepening each day with the realization of death's finality. Dan had said to me before Red died, "I hate death!" with great intensity, with the vehemence that came from deep within him. I thoroughly agreed. Death was the great divider, the inexplicable, unremitting force that took our loved ones away from us . . . and left our hearts raw with pain. Yes, it was Good Friday when Reddy was taken from us, and I wondered, then, holding her in my arms for the last time, what was "good" about it? The Easter scarf around her neck seemed totally incongruous.

The only thing I could do as we left, knowing that Dr. Saam's father had died one and a half weeks before was tell her "I'm sorry for your loss."

Her simple reply, "I'm sorry for yours." No comparing of our sorrows, just a mutual respect for each other's.

FOUR

Easter

The worst part now was the question of what to do with Red's body. After she died in our arms, I didn't want to leave her, but I knew with the ground in my backyard still frozen it was impossible for her to be buried there. I asked Dr. Saam about cremation, telling her there was no way I would leave Red's body if it was just going to be thrown into a heap of dead carcasses, with no guarantee that the ashes I would receive back would be hers. Sensitive to my grief and fears, Dr. Saam assured me and Dan that that would not happen. "When my dog died just recently," she said, "I left his body with the people here. They treat our dead pets' bodies with respect. I never would have left mine unless I was assured of that." That calmed my fears, coming from a person that I had come to know and trust. I still didn't want to leave Red! But what other choice did we have? So Dan and I turned and left her body behind in Dr. Saam's office, one of the hardest things I've ever done. As we left, I glanced back at her inert body lying there on the floor, and prayed to God and the saints that whoever took her remains away treated them respectfully!

I asked Dan if he wanted to go out with me to lunch. He had become very silent, with both of us obviously distraught, but it was after 1:00 in the afternoon and we needed some nourishment. I remembered going out with my brother in Fargo after our dad had died, and finding some strength from each other in our grief. Dan and I drove to Chianti's Grille which was a popular restaurant in the area. We had been there in happier times. This time we pretty much ordered our meals and said very little to each other. Words are inadequate when one is still in shock and overwhelmed with grief. After the meal, Dan had to return to work. We hugged before he left in his car. And then I returned to an empty house. That was awful, a house filled with memories, and a silence that seemed to almost physically hit me with Red's absence.

I spent the afternoon calling JoAnne, our son John, my mother, and some of my closest friends, all of whom gave me their heartfelt sympathy as I told the story of Red's death. My mother, of course, offered her immediate sympathy. She too had loved Red very much, and knew how dear she was to both Dan and me. I remembered, then, after my dad's sudden death, hearing my mother call people she knew, telling them about Dad, and how she seemed to gain strength the more she could share her grief with others. I only felt exhausted, having had so little sleep the night before. I don't remember much that day, except going up to my bedroom, seeing Red's empty kennel there, and being struck by the realization I would never see her again. I wrote in my journal that night before falling asleep, "Red died today at 12:45 p.m. I will miss her terribly!"

The next day was Saturday, "Holy Saturday" in the Christian calendar. All I could think of was Red's dying and our having to leave her body behind. I also thought of how Jesus's disciples must have felt after seeing the death of their friend and teacher, and having his dead body placed in the tomb of Joseph of Arimathea, a man probably few of them knew personally. Again, that Saturday is a blur. Somehow I got through the day by reaching out to other friends by phone, and crying a lot as I did so, my head aching from the sobs. I remember that I kept asking God why Red had died on Good Friday, of all days. Why? What was I supposed to learn from that? Again, I went up the stairs to an empty bedroom, step by step, without my companion who would, when she was in good health, always pass me by as I went up, and wait for me at the top. My journal entry that day was painfully succinct, "God, I miss her so!"

Easter Sunday arrived, with some consolation that Dan had agreed to go with me to the 10:00 o'clock Mass at our parish, St. Stanislaus. The priest there, Father Clay, is a very lovable Irish man whose homilies seem to always have the same message, "God loves us—no matter what." I didn't care so much whether God did love us; it didn't seem like a loving God would take away a beautiful dog who had brought Dan and me and so many others so much happiness. And I wasn't all that sure I loved God. There certainly was no joy in resurrection for Dan and me. Although Easter Sunday was meant to be a reminder of life in the midst of death, I felt nauseous. The beauty of the Easter lilies surrounding the altar only reminded me of the beautiful dog who had just died in my arms. For me, Red was gone and her absence seemed overwhelming.

I did pray again that she was not alone in the spirit world, and that my dad and my father-in-law Mel were caring for her after her own transition to another reality. This spontaneous prayer, preceded by my words to her when she died, was the beginning, I think, of an innate, intuitive, yet unarticulated belief that animals too must have souls. Why should we think that only we humans might be favored with God's loving presence after death, if, in fact, God was a loving being?

At this time, though, on Easter Sunday, I was experiencing the second stage of what Elizabeth Kubler-Ross describes as typical of those facing the death of someone we love, stages of denial, anger, bargaining, depression, and acceptance. These stages Kubler-Ross saw as applying to people grieving human deaths; I, came to see, with my own grief process, them applying very much to the loss of a beloved pet as well. The first stage, denial, was expressed in my failure to see how sick she was initially and my inability to accept that she was going to die. The second stage was manifest in my anger, Easter Sunday, not only at God but at the saints, Brigit, and Francis especially, to whom I had prayed and who had left me, I felt, bereft. Only later would I begin to realize that perhaps it was their prayers that gave Red three more months of life. Yes, certainly my attentiveness helped and the medication she received, but for at least that short amount of time she regained her appetite, vitality, energy . . . until the last weeks. I had done what I could to save her. My only consolation later was that I'd tried; my sense of desolation now came with the awareness that though she and Dan and I had won the initial battles, we had lost the war.

In the days ahead, though, after Easter Sunday, my anger turned to rage that nothing seems to last, and behind the rage my fear that I might lose another loved one in my life. My grieving the loss of Reddy had somehow constellated other griefs and losses—past and anticipatory—and the fear that *this* God in whom I had believed is instead like the grim-reaper, perhaps desiring to take everything and everyone I loved. JoAnne had told me on various occasions, "Life is fragile." Now, once again, that was confirmed; that we are all vulnerable, humans and animals alike, to death whenever it might come! I thought of the stories of near-death survivors, and how they often heard a voice telling them to return to life, because their time "was not yet up." Well, who decides that, and why? Both my father and Mel, my father-in-law who was like a second father to me after my dad's death, had died young. Red who had always been indispensable was now gone, the one who always kept me company watching television or reading, whose presence gave me comfort and joy. Mark Doty writes in his memoir on the death of his dogs, how "death leaves me furious, sorrowing . . ." I felt that: furious, rageful, angry at God!

And now, with Red's death, I also encountered aloneness for the first time in my life. I had always had my family, friends, community, JoAnne, our boys, my dear dog—and now, with JoAnne still living in the other house and being totally immersed in her work, I had no one to come home to! Emptiness, loneliness, and, yes, a powerful sense of abandonment! Again, as Doty has written, dogs are "a sort of cure for our great, abiding loneliness. A temporary cure, but a real one." Without Red, I now knew what real loneliness was when I entered an empty house.

Kubler-Ross's third stage, bargaining, didn't seem to apply. I had nothing left to bargain with or for. One interpretation of that stage is associated with feelings of "if only," if only I had done something differently. I didn't feel that way. I had done everything within my capacity to attend to her sickness, once it was discovered. God knows I had taken her as soon as I recognized how thin she had become, first to Dr. Wheeler in the Eagan clinic and then to the University of Minnesota's animal hospital and Dr. Saam. I had done everything they advised me to do, paid for all the medical sessions, as well as the medications and special dogfood. Only the day she died was she diagnosed with cancer. Even if they had diagnosed it earlier, I doubt if they could have done anything to stop its spread. No, it was the next stage of grief, depression that took over my life after Easter.

Depression settled in for what seemed a long, long time as the finality of death set in: the dawning realization that I would never see Red again in this life. A great emptiness in the house when I returned after teaching, especially at night when the house echoed emptiness without her. I longed to hear and see her charging down the steps in the morning, happily looking forward to *another day.* I longed to hear her bark of outrage at the mailman or anyone passing by within earshot. I longed to see her once more at the door with her tail wagging as I returned from teaching or my other numerous meetings. Now there were to be no more days with Reddy—only silence in the house. No wonder I longed for a dream or dreams of her. But they never came; only dreams in the weeks that followed her death of moonscapes, iguanas, and conflicts with colleagues. *I wanted to see her once more!* Especially as I started having difficulties in remembering what she looked like, as if her images were fading from my mind. I would ask, how can this be happening?

The weather, after Red died, reinforced my depression and anger. Winter returned in April, not an unusual occurrence in Minnesota, but, as the newspaper reported, it was "the longest stretch below 50 degrees in April in 28 years." The cold weather was accompanied, of course, with more precipitation. The new snow on trees and branches perhaps any other time might have been appreciated for its clean and sparkling beauty. Now it only added to my pain, the pain of death, of separation. When I entered my house, I would still call out her name when she was alive, "Reddy, I'm home," but there was, of course, no dog running to meet me! I would still put food out on her plate, a small offering in her empty bowl of things she loved that I had denied to her while she was sick. I'd heard about this custom in my reading and my travels to Asia, how for a certain period of time a family would remember the one who had died by leaving them offerings of food. (Only my friend Kenny, a Korean-American, immediately recognized what I was doing when he visited. He had done it for his ancestors, a gesture his parents from Korea had taught him.) In the midst of this, I was also feeling a great deal of ambivalence: *not* wanting to be with people, and *not* wanting to be alone. Dan told me he felt the same way.

The first time I went for a walk without Red was so very difficult. I had avoided going out; I did not want to do it without her! I remembered our last walk together when she only could go half a block and I had to pick her up and carry her home. On this first walk without her there were signs of spring finally emerging from the bleakness of winter, but the coldness of winter still prevailed for me. I set out with her leash crammed in my coat-pocket, something I could hold onto, but that others wouldn't be able to see. As I walked, I saw other people with their dogs, and I felt jealous and hurt, remembering my walks with Reddy. As I passed the familiar sights around the neighborhood on the route we always took after our move to Asbury, I was almost home when I met a neighbor lady, someone whom I really didn't know all that well. As I was making my way down the sidewalk, about to cross the street where my house was, I ran into her. Seeing me, she spontaneously asked, obviously with no knowledge of Red's death, "how are you?" Just a polite inquiry, but I burst into tears.

"This is my first walk," I stammered, "without my dog Red. She just died last week and I miss her so . . . "

Along with the sense of death's finality came guilt. Guilt, I learned after my father's death, often accompanies our grief. In the weeks following Dad's death I was filled with remorse, memories of times I had treated him poorly, when I had fought with him as a teenager, when, as a young adult, I had argued with him about the war in Vietnam that seemed would never end. One argument, in particular, about my wire-rim glasses and the length of my hair, had not ended well. He had asked me what people in Wyndmere, the small town in North Dakota where he and Mom lived, "would think?" I had told him, "I don't give a damn what they think," and then the words I later regretted, "I wish you had never been my father!" That episode came back to haunt me, after he died, even though, thankfully, I had asked his forgiveness and we had reconciled over that. But after he died I had felt tremendous guilt.

Now with Red's death, I remembered how I had treated her as a puppy, trying to housebreak her, and my impatience with her on our first walks. I remembered the time before I had moved out of our house on Princeton; how I'd let her out at night in our backyard, and, despite my calls, she had refused to come back in. Perhaps she had seen something, a rabbit or squirrel. But because I had to go out and get her when she didn't come into the house, I had gone out and grabbed her and then spanked her very hard. I was under tension with the move and all that was going on, but I beat her for what I perceived as her stubbornness. (She, as was usual with her in so many difficult and painful circumstances, accepted it without fighting back, or growling, or whining!) I remembered her loud and plaintive howl when I moved her to our new house on Asbury, obviously a difficult change for her, accompanied I am sure by bewilderment!

Depressed and feeling guilty, I joined a grief group just five days after her death, sponsored by the University of Minnesota Animal Hospital where Red had died. Dr. Saam had told me about it; how sessions had been set up for all those grieving the loss of their pets who wanted to help them recover, and there was no charge. This group met every other week on Wednesday nights for an hour and a half. I initially felt uncomfortable when I went there for the first time. Weren't men supposed to hide their feelings, and not be so vulnerable about expressing them? A number of participants acknowledged how they felt a bit crazy to be so affected by their loss while others in their families seemed to move on with their lives quite quickly. Each of us started the session by introducing ourselves and telling about the animal that had brought us there. Depending on how recent our loss, the emotions expressed were often quite raw and tissues were passed around freely. When it was my turn, I started telling the group about Reddy, and pretty much broke down.

In this group, all of us knew the love we had for our animals, and understood from first-hand experience the depth of grief that had entered our lives. I felt comforted when I left. All of us benefited, it seemed, from our finding a group that did not make judgments as we shared our stories and expressed our feelings. Our facilitator of the group, Jeannine Moga, was exceptionally helpful in encouraging us to share what we felt while at the same time being sensitive when some in the group were not ready to open up. Highly insightful, sensitive, and compassionate, she acknowledged in one of the sessions that she was in her profession precisely because she had experienced similar losses as ourselves. Only in one of the later sessions did she actually make me feel uncomfortable, however, when I shared my fear and guilt that perhaps I was somehow responsible for Red's death. Had my move to Asbury and the disruption that went with it caused her "early" demise? (Again, I remembered her howl!) Rather than mitigating my fear, Jeannine acknowledged that sometimes major changes can adversely affect an animal's health. Then I was really overwhelmed with guilt! Something that I added to my list. (Only later was this somewhat resolved when I acknowledged to myself that if I was responsible for Red's demise, I never intended to cause that with our move.)

Another side of me, as the weeks unfolded after Red's death, was the growing desire to find another dog. I told myself that a person should not just go out and replace one beautiful dog with another in order to deal with the sharp edges of grief and loneliness. No, I reminded myself, grief must be experienced rather than unacknowledged or cut short. I told myself that I was not ready yet; I have to grieve my loss of Red first before I'd have room in my heart for another dog. My grief group at the hospital with Jeannine was helping a great deal, but still I hated the empty house! Now was the time, I realized, that I needed to sit with my grief, to remember Red, before moving on to a new life without her. I knew this, but I didn't like it. Red was a family member, not just a possession.

In the midst of this grief, I called Carol Juelfs, Red's groomer, to whom I had dropped off flowers after Easter Sunday Mass as a gift for all that she had done for Red. She told me, over the phone, how "the tulips you left me lasted the longest I've ever seen." Then, trying to be helpful, she said: "I know it will be hard to find another animal like Red. She had the sweetest disposition, patience, and calm temperament. But I know a man who has a beautiful English cocker spaniel whom I think you should meet, and he may help you find another." I told her I would like that—but not right now.

Monday, April 23rd, two and a half weeks after leaving Red's body in Dr. Saam's office, I received a phone call from a young woman who said her name was Leslie, telling me that Red's ashes were ready to be picked up. That news was hard enough to hear, although I was anxious to get them and give them a proper burial. It was the *happy* tone of her voice on a Monday morning, however, and the way she sounded as if it was like picking up a box of chocolates that I wanted to throttle her! My Red, my beloved dog, so full of life and energy and love—reduced now to a small container of ashes! Oh, God, how hard that was to comprehend OR accept. When I drove back to the hospital where Red had died and went in to pick up her ashes, the young woman at the desk—not Leslie— was more sympathetic. "I'm sorry for your loss," she said quietly when handing over the box of ashes. I looked at the accompanying certificate of authenticity: Red had been cremated on Friday the 13th, one week after Good Friday. How appropriate I thought, long equating the date with bad luck! Leaving the hospital with Red's ashes, I broke into sobs when I reached a place of safety where no one could observe my tears. The total incomprehensibility again: there was no way Red was there in that small cardboard box! She was so much more than any physical remains!

The same day I took Red's ashes home with me, I received an email from Peter Freeman, the man with a dog Carol had wanted me to meet. Synchronicity, I wondered? He introduced himself as a professor at the College of St. Thomas and, like myself, said he had a "background in Jungian thought and practice." He went on say: "I heard through Carol that you recently suffered the loss of your cocker spaniel. My condolences for sure. She thought you might be interested in meeting my English Cocker Spaniel, Baxter, and hear about my breeder. If you would be willing and are interested in coffee sometime, drop me a line." I put it aside, thinking again that I was not yet ready for that.

But I did start visiting the dog pound not far from my house where dogs were kept until they found a home—if they were lucky! I'd look in at the cages with the dogs of various breeds looking up at me, some wagging their tails, hoping for an encouraging word; some withdrawn, depressed, hiding from my gaze. I observed two really cute puppies playing together, and an older dog fighting valiantly to not be returned to the kennel; all of them begging to be loved. I wanted to help all them escape this incarceration. I wanted to bring them all home with me! (But when I told Dan, he suggested that probably wouldn't be a good idea!) With the permission of the staff, I'd take one or two on walks in the nearby park which they obviously enjoyed, getting out of their confinement. They reminded me of the great desire humans and animals share, to belong somewhere, to be loved, to find a home—and I'd feel so guilty returning them—all of them desperate for love, yet crying out to me, "We're not Red." Once again I was reminded of the great loss I had so recently experienced. Plus I would remember her fierce barking at me—and the puppy, Shell, that Dan had brought home unexpectedly whom Reddy perceived as an interloper into my affections and *her* house. I didn't think she would yet accept another dog.

Besides the visits to the dog pound, in the weeks that followed I began to rely upon certain resources and rituals for help in dealing with my anger, depression, guilt, loneliness, and overwhelming grief. Just ten days after Red's death, on April 16th, I had begun writing notes about her. It was spontaneous, as had been the writing of what eventually became a book, *Father and Son: Time*

Lost, Love Recovered, after my father died. I had begun jotting notes as I drove back home, after Dad's funeral Mass and burial, with JoAnne and John and Dan in the car with me. At one point, JoAnne (always subtle) had said to me, "why don't you write later, before you kill us all?" Writing notes on Red was just as spontaneous after she had died, originating in my being a writer, my need to write, to begin to tell her story as I had done after my father's death, and experience, in doing so, a way of finding solace. For both my dad and Red, this spontaneous writing their stories was an act of love.

Certainly, another significant resource was my having the grief group I had joined and continued to rely upon. Each time we met and got to know each other better, friendship between us grew and a sense of communion from which each of us received comfort and greater healing. However, the more times we met the more I wanted to do a Fourth and Fifth Step with Jeannine because of her sensitivity and compassion. She knew about these steps she said, both of which were part of the Twelve Steps of Alcoholics Anonymous which had originally been written by Bill Wilson, a founder of AA, for alcoholics' own path to recovery. Step Four, "Made a searching and fearless moral inventory of ourselves," preceded Step Five, "Admitted to God, to ourselves and to another human being the exact nature of our wrongs." The two of them went together and, from my Catholic upbringing, I saw them in many ways as similar to an extended examination of conscience and a general confession of one's wrongs. I was familiar with all Twelve Steps in my work with recovering chemically dependent people when I had worked as a counselor before becoming a theologian and had listened to many Fifth Steps. In my clinical training at Hazelden Rehabilitation Center in Minnesota the Fifth Step I took was so healing for me that I wanted to study it more. As a result, my doctoral dissertation at Notre Dame had been a comparative study of the Roman Catholic sacrament of penance and AA's Fifth Step. Now, after losing Red, and being filled with so much regret and guilt, I asked Jeannine to listen to my Fifth Step, focusing it on my relationship with my beloved dog. When I met with her in her office four weeks after Red's death, I told her of my feelings of guilt and regret as they related to dear Reddy: the times I had been mean to her, starting with that walk as a puppy. Jeannine listened well and guided me in my confession of those hurtful acts for which I felt so much guilt, and as a result I did experience a sense of relief and release when I finished. We sat in silence for a while, and then she asked me the poignant question, "Now that you've completed your step, do you think Red has forgiven you?"

It was so unexpected that I had to pause, and then blurt out, "I hope so. I loved her dearly, and I believe she loved me too, and knew at the end of her life how much she meant to me. Yes, I think she forgives me. The hard part, of course, is learning to forgive myself." That would take much longer.

Another resource in my process of healing was the ritual I planned for Red as a memorial dinner Sunday, May 6th, exactly a month after her death. JoAnne thought it was a good idea too. We invited those family members who were especially close to Red: JoAnne's brother, Greg, and his wife, Bobbie, who had taken such a keen interest in how Red was trained and always demonstrated her love for Red as she grew older. JoAnne and Dan, were there, of course; John was studying for finals, and couldn't make it. The five of us gathered in the new house at 4:00 in the afternoon. It was a simple memorial service. I lit a candle in my study where a picture of Red was placed, and we all sat around it. Starting with a prayer for Red, I then had each of us read a short excerpt from various books, pausing for quiet reflection after each of them. Bobbie started with a short quotation from Anatole France, "Until one has loved an animal, a part of one's soul remains unawakened." Greg read from a saying by Standing Bear, a Lakota chief and civil rights leader:

> If a man could prove to some bird or animal that he was a worthy friend it would share with him precious secrets and there would be formed bonds of loyalty never to be broken; the man would protect the rights and life of the animal, and the animal would share with the man his power, skill, and wisdom. In this manner was the great

brotherhood of mutual helpfulness formed, adding to the reverence for life other than man.

Dan's reading was from Juliette Wood's *The Celtic Book of Living and Dying*:

> More than just a source of food, clothing and transport, animals had an intense spiritual significance for the Celts. Many creatures were thought to possess supernatural powers of special wisdom, and to be able to move freely between the everyday realm and the Otherworld . . . The loyalty of dogs makes them the most beloved of domestic animals, but they are also healing symbols, and they are often associated with the Otherworld.

JoAnne's was from Henry Beston's *Outermost House*:

> We need another and a wiser and perhaps a more mythical concept of animals. . . .. We patronize them for their incompleteness, for their tragic fate of having taken form so far below ourselves. And therein we err, and greatly err. For the animals shall not be measured by man. In a world older and more complete than ours they moved finished and complete, gifted with extensions of the senses we have lost or never attained, living by voices we shall never hear. They are not brethren, they are not underlings; they are other nations caught with ourselves in the net of life and time, fellow prisoners of the splendor and travail of the earth.

My reading was from Mark Doty's *Dog Years*:

> One of the unspoken truths of American life is how deeply people grieve over the animals who live and die with them, how real their emptiness is, how profound the silence is these creatures leave in their wake. Our culture expects us not only to bear these losses alone, but to be ashamed of how deeply we feel them.

Once these readings were completed and the time for quiet reflection that followed each, I asked everyone, one by one, to tell a story about Red that came to mind. These spontaneous stories were often quite humorous, remembering some of her adventures as a puppy, her love of parties, her barking at the mailman. Sometimes they were sad as we recalled how much we missed her. It was a lively conversation, one story leading into another as we recalled, as one person said, Red's "joyous soul" and how much joy she had brought each of us. This simple ritual closed with another prayer, one of thanksgiving for all that she had given us, and was followed by a dinner in her honor. JoAnne made her special *red* cake in Red's honor that we shared for dessert.

I continued teaching classes, in the midst of all these activities associated with the loss of Red. The end of the semester was finally in sight with my last class May 10th. Before then, however, I had finally met Peter Freeman with his dog, Baxter, at Carol's house. I was so impressed with his beautiful black cocker spaniel, and realized if I was to bring another dog into my life, I wanted it to be that breed. Two days after the memorial dinner at the house on Asbury Street, Peter and I met again for coffee at 9:30 in the morning in a nearby coffee shop. It was then that Peter gave me the address and phone number of the breeder from whom he had gotten Baxter. I told him I wanted to contact the breeder to see if she had any dogs that were multi-colored. I didn't want another red cocker that would remind me of Reddy. A short time after our coffee I called the number Peter had given me. I had decided I needed another puppy in my life. My son Daniel had already, while JoAnne was still in our house on Princeton, gotten a Rottweiler puppy whom he named "Angel" to keep him company.

We didn't bury Red's ashes until Monday, May 14th. My classes were done, and signs of spring were everywhere, from the beautiful purple lilacs on the trees, hanging over the fence in our backyard on Asbury Street, to the yellow daffodils bursting into bloom in the front yard that symbolize, it is said, rebirth and new beginnings. Though not sunflowers as in Vincent Van Gogh's paintings, the color yellow as he depicted them also symbolizes joy and bonds of friendship. It was my friend Bill who said to me after hearing of Red's death, "Well, she was your soul-mate, your soul-friend, really," confirming what I had written about in my own books, describing a soul friend as someone with whom we have a deep friendship, one that survives death itself. All of the spring weather too had lightened my grief a bit, as I looked out the windows of my new porch that had been built the autumn before Red's sickness and dying. Though Easter had been such a depressing time dealing with Red's death on Good Friday, the different activities in which I had sought comfort afterwards—from the grief group to the Fifth Step to the memorial dinner—were helping me begin to feel a sense of resurrection. I remembered the kindness of friends, the cookies JoAnne made for me, the flowers she brought to the new house, the condolences of my mother. Not that I would ever be done with grieving Red's absence, but I would also remember all that Red had given to so many people, especially Dan and me. Resurrection, finding life in the midst of death is a long process, I thought; one like the disciples experienced in which the healing of grief never completely ends the feelings of loss and the deep longing to see the ones whom we love who are physically absent.

Daniel came over to my house that afternoon for the burial of Red's ashes. We took turns digging a hole in my backyard, near the northern side of the fence where eventually a Celtic cross JoAnne had given me had the word "Red" added to its base by Bill, marking where she was buried. Then, as Dan held the box of ashes in his hands, I blessed them, recalling all that Red had done for us in making us so happy. I blessed them with holy water, and ended with the prayer, "Rest in peace, dear Reddy." As we finished covering with dirt the box containing her ashes, I told Dan, "When I die, please dig them up and bury them with me."

Dan, already distraught, replied with tears in his eyes, "Yes, Dad, I will. But I don't want to talk about it right now!"

I set out two days later, after the burial of Red's ashes, for Wisconsin to bring home another cocker spaniel puppy. It was to be a four-hour drive going there and of course another four returning. Dan asked me, "Are you crazy? You haven't even seen a picture of her!" Days before, I had received a call from the Sharon Reimann, the breeder, telling me that she had a beautiful white and brown and black puppy for sale. She called just an hour after I had had a talk with Reddy, telling her, "I love you, Reddy; you will never be replaced, and I will never forget you, but I need another dog in my life, another puppy!" Within an hour of that talk with Red, I received a phone call from Sharon telling me that a multi-colored puppy was now for sale. She was an English cocker like Baxter; bred to be a show dog, but when she hadn't grown large enough, they decided to sell her to a deserving person. Yes, I was interested, I told Sharon, and, after ending our conversation, I thanked Red, and God, for the synchronicity!

I set out, then, six weeks after Red's death, on Wednesday, May 16th, to purchase a puppy that I only knew from a brief verbal description given to me by Sharon. But I had a great deal of hope that this puppy was meant for me, and that Reddy approved. The four hours went quickly, as I listened to the car radio and stopped for a quick lunch at a McDonalds. As I got closer to the actual farm, I became lost briefly on a dirt road, but then found my way. Sharon met me as I stopped the car in front of her house, introduced herself, and then took me to the kennel. There were a number of dogs in the enclosure, but she reached down and picked up a bundle of fur, and set the puppy on the ground in front of me. There she was, looking up at me, and wagging her butt back and forth rapidly. (Hence, her later nickname, "Wiggle-butt"!) I picked her up and held her in my arms, squirming a bit, but obviously nervous. Sharon said, "Oh, look, she's excited to see you."

"No," I said, "she's scared." (Again, as I would discover later, that puppy was an introvert compared to Red's being an extrovert or party girl.) I held her for a while, and looked into her dark eyes, and thought, "she's not Reddy, but she is beautiful!" I told Sharon, "Yes, I do want her. Let's sign the papers so I can take her home."

The trip back went quickly with my new puppy huddled in the box with a comfortable cushion on which she slept. Again, being an introvert, she wasn't really wanting to look around—as Reddy had done on my drive back from the farm where we had found her with Dan holding her on his lap. We arrived back at Asbury Street after dark. I carried her into the kitchen and put her down on the floor. She looked around, and went into the dining room and living room where my fireplace was. She looked at herself in the glass door of the fireplace, just as Reddy had done when I first brought her into her and my new house. Then I took her upstairs where my study was, and she did a curious thing, walking over to the small altar I had there with Reddy's collar on it next to her picture. She went directly to it and then sniffed it, seeming to know and acknowledge that she was coming into a home that had already been blessed by another loving dog.

FIVE

Muse

I named the new puppy "Hana," after the picturesque Road to Hana on the island of Maui, my favorite of the Hawaiian islands. Eventually I found myself calling her "Hana Lee" at times, evidently influenced subconsciously by the song of Peter, Paul, and Mary, "Puff the Magic Dragon," popular in the 1960s, in whose lyrics are found "the land of Honahlee." Hana brought a renewed sense of joy in my life. Like Reddy, she was there when I got home after teaching; unlike Red whom I had put in a kennel at night for years, precisely because someone had told me dogs really appreciated being there, I put Hana in bed with me. Yes, the first time was somewhat traumatic since she didn't know it was a bed and proceeded to relieve herself there! That changed, after hearing my cries of alarm! Hana is a jewel with her beautiful colors, her demure personality, her wiggle-butt. But the grief I felt with Reddy's death did not, of course, totally end with Hana's presence.

I continued to go to the grief group at the University of Minnesota's Animal Hospital for the next couple months after Hana's arrival, and participated that fall, on October 6th, in an Interfaith Animal Blessing and Memorial Ceremony, organized by Jeannine. It took place in an open field on the hospital grounds, and all those who had suffered the loss of a pet the past year were invited to bring a picture or some memento of their dead pet. If we cared to do so, we could also bring our new pets for a blessing. I took a picture of Red for the ceremony and Hana came with me on a leash. According to the program we all received, "this event was created to provide animal lovers with an opportunity to publicly honor the important animal relationships in their lives as well as to hold healing space for those grieving the loss of a loved animal." On a stage in the open field were representatives from various religious or spiritual traditions involved in the program with the rest of us gathered around it. The representatives included an Episcopal priest, a Native American shaman, a Jewish rabbi, a Buddhist monk, and a Catholic priest.

The service began with a cleansing of the area with burning sage and sweet grass by the shaman, followed by a "Thunderdrum" which was to call the spirits of the deceased animals. Let's just say the Thunderdrum lived up to its name as its loud vibrations, like thunder, echoed across the field, resulting in Hana and other dogs barking loudly as it was beaten. This was followed with opening remarks and a welcome by Jeannine, a short homily by the Episcopal priest, and a blessing of all animal "guests" we had brought. The latter action took place as various ministers, including the shaman, went from one person and/or animal to another, blessing the picture, the memento, and the pet itself. Being a shy dog, Hana did not like the Thunderdrum nor the shaman who approached her, and, if she had not been on a leash held by me, I'm sure she would have left the premises immediately. As it were, the shaman blessed the picture of Red and my quivering puppy. A mike had been set up in the field so that, after the blessing, anyone could go to it and tell a story of their dearly-departed pet. The program stated that "stories are an important part of healing ritual in every culture, whether we are the storytellers or the witnesses." Following that, we were all invited to light a candle in honor of our pets. The program ended with a Buddhist prayer, a Jewish prayer, and a benediction. The Jewish prayer was especially moving:

> In the rising of the sun and in its going down,
>   we remember them.
> In the flowing of the wind and in the chill of winter,

we remember them.
In the opening of buds and in the rebirth of spring,
    we remember them.
In the blueness of the sky and in the warmth of summer,
    we remember them.
In the rustling leaves and in the beauty of autumn,
    we remember them.
In the beginning of the year and when it ends,
    we remember them.
When we are weary and in need of strength,
    we remember them.
When we are lost and sick at heart,
    we remember them.
When we have joys we yearn to share,
    we remember them.
So long as we live they too shall live,
        for they are now a part of us,
        as we remember them.

During the last prayers, many of us noticed far out on the horizon an object of some kind flying towards where we were gathered. Jeannine had the closing remarks, but since she and all the presenters were facing us, none of them observed the bird which was approaching from behind them. As it flew closer, we realized that the bird was a magnificent eagle with its wings floating on the wind. Some of us began pointing into the sky as it drew closer, and finally Jeannine turned to see it, as we all did, circle three times and then retreat. It seemed to many of us as some sort of blessing bestowed on us by another creature, honoring all those who had died that year as well as those living animals accompanying us that day. Many of us were in tears as it flew away! After the conclusion of the program with this dramatic ending, I went up to Jeannine to thank her for organizing such a wonderful service, introduce Hana to her, and then say, "Wow! That eagle was something else! Did you arrange for it show up when it did?" We laughed, and she said she was as surprised as we were at its appearance.

Later that day, I had my good Irish friend Patrick Shaeffer over for a drink (or two) so that I could introduce him to Hana.

He took one look at her and referring to her long nose said, "She looks just like a mallard!"

"Ah, shut up!! I said. Then I told him of the dramatic conclusion of the memorial service, with the eagle flying overhead.

He seemed less impressed with my story, shall we say, when he responded, "Well, of course that might happen. An eagle seeing all those animals in an open field; of course, he's going to come and inspect what might be a meal or two!"

I coughed up the Jameson that I was drinking, and told him, "You bastard! How to ruin a good thing!"

We could laugh together at his (somewhat) humorous response. But his friendship was one of the reasons, along with Hana herself that helped relieve to some degree the grief that continued in my life. Other friends contributed too. In the days and weeks and months following Red's death, my son and I were surprised how kind and understanding people seemed to be, not judging our grief with words like "it was only a dog," or "you can get another pet." Both of us were initially reticent about sharing our grief, but relieved when so many people's response was that of immediate sympathy and understanding. My friend, Jim Rogers' comment helped a great deal when he said, "It took me three weeks before I stopped crying when I lost my dog."

The cards that Dan and I received from family and friends were consoling as well. My mom sent a card to both Dan and me that had a beautiful forest scene with a river running through it on the cover, and the words:

> In their eyes
> You saw a loving soul,
> and in your heart
> You knew you'll never
> have a finer friend.

Inside the card:

> Deepest sympathies
> in the loss of your pet
> who meant so much.

And the message in Mom's own handwriting:

Dearest Eddie and Danny,
I, too, feel so badly
That Red had to die

—Love you, Mom and Grandma

Another card I received which meant a lot came from the veterinarian Karen Wheeler who had treated Red for years before she sent her to the University Animal Hospital. On its cover was a red heart with black footprints walking across it, with a quotation of Eleanor Roosevelt's:

Many will walk in
and out of your life . . .
but only friends will
leave footprints in your heart.

And inside Karen had written:

Mr. Sellner, I am so very sorry about Red. I will always remember her as one of the sweetest cockers to walk through the clinic doors. It was obvious she was well-loved, and also she, herself, loved so very well. Take care.

A former student of mine, Maureen O'Brien, also sent a sympathy card with the handwritten note:

You taught me a spirituality course over ten years ago. I know you probably don't remember me, but I remember in the class telling us funny stories about the cocker spaniel puppy you'd just gotten and decided to name "Red." I am so sorry to hear of Red's death. I'm a "pet person." I had dogs growing up and now, as an adult, I have cats. I know saying goodbye does not get easier, but I firmly believe that one day we will be united again with our beloved companion animals. You are in my thoughts and prayers.

Maureen was someone I hadn't seen for such a long time, and it was especially moving to me that she would have remembered my stories about Reddy in a course I taught many years before when Dan and I had just brought her home as a puppy. Other more recent students, of course, did know about her sickness and then her death, since I couldn't help but share with them my anxiety about her initially and my grief when she died, especially those last weeks before summer began. I still had to teach a graduate course on Jungian psychology and spiritual direction the first part of the summer following Red's death, but then was happy I could take a break from my teaching. By the time classes started again in the fall, I found myself returning to the questions her death had raised.

First of all, I was still haunted by the question of why she had to die on Good Friday. As a Catholic theologian, I couldn't ignore the synchronicity of her death on the very day Jesus had died on the cross. What was the meaning of that? I didn't consider it just chance. Other questions also arose. Is there life after death for beloved animals? How could I reconcile the theology that I had been taught as a Catholic that animals do not have souls and therefore do not have a life after death—with my very real sense that there had to be more to Red's life than that? From the time of her death, I believed that she still survived on another level of existence. Despite what I had been taught about animals, I still had spontaneously prayed for my dad and Mel to take care of Red. I had also carried on conversations with her after she died about whether I should get another puppy. I believed too that she helped me find Hana when I did. Beyond this, her death also raised questions about God: whether God really existed or if God did exist, what sort of God he or she might be. These experiences and beliefs led me beyond reason into the realm of the heart. They took me into that part of our nature inclusive of the very important dimensions of intuition and affects, and into the spiritual realities of faith, hope, and love.

I discovered that I wasn't alone in my questioning. The pamphlet Jeannine had given me when I joined the grief group, *Coping with the Loss of Your Companion Animal,* had mentioned in the section on "Manifestations of Grief" common elements that many people experienced, such as "feeling angry at God when loss occurs, renewed or shaken religious beliefs, questioning whether or not souls exist and wondering what happens to loved ones after death." A book I purchased not long after Red's death, *Finding Comfort after the Loss of Your Animal Friend*, by Allen and Linda Anderson, affirmed what I was feeling: "Our animal's passing evokes questions about the significance of the animal-human relationship, the afterlife, the soul, and God. Your longing to find answers, explanations, and consolation may bring you to a spiritual turning-point." My questions and my search to answer them were having that effect.

I began reading as much as I could on animals, on the question of whether they had souls, on what sort of God I believed in. It was as if Reddy was now leading me in a totally new direction in my theology and spirituality, my teaching and my writing, as she had led me to the bluff overlooking the Mississippi and to the icon in my study ablaze with light. In the months and years following her death she became my spirit guide, as she had been when alive, and my muse after her death as I began to research and write about animals and spirituality. For Red's illness and death not only opened up theological questions, but an entire world of which I knew little, if anything about at the time: the world of animals, of animal hospitals, of humane societies dedicated to relieving the neglect, abuse, and suffering of animals, of people who have grieved or are grieving the loss of a beloved pet, of books on grief and loss; a world of anguish, empathy, and wonderment.

First, I began to pursue the theological questions raised by Red's death: what happens to beloved animals when they die? Does their spirit live on; certainly in memory, but in reality? Do they have souls? And, pursuing these questions, I was led back to the question, if one believes in God, what sort of God that might be.

Christian writers have, I discovered, wrestled with these questions over the centuries. All go back to Jesus himself, of course, and the values he taught his followers; this Jesus who was born in a stable, most likely surrounded by animals (cf. Luke 2:1–20). His world, before his public ministry took him to Jerusalem, was primarily rural, close to nature, to the lakes and the Sea of Galilee and the desert as well. An observant man, he certainly would have been aware of animals in every form being part of the landscape. He seems to have appreciated this natural world, and loved it, all of creation, seeing God's love as inclusive of the lilies of the field, the birds of the air, and especially all those who are suffering (cf. Luke 13:34; Matt 6:26ff.). In grieving over the fate of Jerusalem, he revealed his empathy and compassion toward animals, identifying *himself* as a mother hen who wants to gather her chicks to protect them (Matt 23:37–39). Still, according to the canonical gospels (those recognized by the Church as fully inspired, that is, Matthew, Mark, Luke, and John) he did not preach specifically about the treatment of animals or their destiny. But he knew about suffering, and taught his disciples the need for being compassionate *toward all* who suffered, teachings especially reflected in his Beatitudes and Sermon on the Mount (Matt 5–7). His own theology had been taught to him through the early sacred writings of his people, the Hebrew scriptures, revealing the teachings that God had made a covenant "with *all* living creatures" (Gen 9:8–17), that "righteous" people care for their animals (Prov 12:10), and that God is a friend of the poor, the downtrodden, the homeless, and all who suffer. These were lessons taught to him by Isaiah, one of the prophets he highly identified with, considering how frequently his followers quoted the prophet in their own writings. Jesus also had learned of the awareness of God's care for all creation in the psalms, including Psalm 36:

> Your love, Lord, reaches to the heavens,
> your truth to the skies.
> Your justice is like the mountains of God,
> your judgments like the deep.
>
> Lord, protector of mortals and beasts,
> how precious, God, is your love.
> Hence, the children of the earth
> find refuge in the shelter of your wings.

So there are intimations, in the canonical writings, of the personality and teachings of Jesus, of his belief in an all-loving God who, like a father, had created the universe and cared for all creatures. In the "apocryphal" gospels (those written at the same time or later than those recognized as canonical), however, I found stories that were much more explicit about Jesus and his relationship with animals. Though the Gospel of Luke does not specifically mention animals being present at the time of Jesus's birth, in the apocryphal Gospel of Pseudo-Matthew, the description of Jesus's birth specifically includes the presence of animals (the ox, donkey, and sheep), thus depicting something of the iconic Peaceable Kingdom where humans and animals live in harmony and peace, inferred in the writings of Isaiah and Hosea. Other animal stories appear in these writings. While the Gospel of Matthew has Jesus referring to "the birds in the sky" which "do not sow or reap or gather into barns; yet your heavenly Father feeds them" (Matt 6:25–26), in the apocryphal Gospel of Thomas Jesus, at the age of five, actually creates sparrows (twelve of them), causing some controversy because he did so on the Sabbath.

In another Coptic text there is a story of Jesus who found a man beating his over-loaded mule, and confronts him: "Man, why do you beat your animal? Do you not see that it is too weak for its burden, and do you not know that it suffers pains? Do you not see how it bleeds, and do you not hear how it groans and cries out for mercy? From now on then, do not beat it anymore, so that you too may find mercy." In another story, from the Gospel of Pseudo-Matthew, Jesus encounters on the road to Jericho young lions who come out of a cave and run around his feet, playing with him, while their mother and other older lions bow their heads and worship him. As a result of this, Jesus preached to the people who had gathered there: "How much better are the beasts than you, seeing that they recognize their Lord and glorify him; while you, made in the image and likeness of God, do not know him!" This teaching of Jesus, implying the spiritual superiority of animals in recognizing and worshipping him in contrast to humans, was and still is an extraordinary idea, since the common view throughout later centuries of Christian thought was that humans were superior to animals precisely because humans were made in the image of God!

So in these apocryphal writings Jesus is much more explicitly portrayed than in the canonical writings as a lover of animals, defender of them, compassionate toward them, someone who considered them fellow-creatures, even superior to humankind in spiritual awarenesses. I was amazed at this view of Jesus as a lover and protector of animals, and I was encouraged by it as I thought of Red with her attributes of unconditional love and compassion, and how she had graced my life and my son Daniel's.

As I studied more of the history of Christian theology in relation to animals, I discovered the opposite view emerging, the one I had been raised with that is so highly detrimental to animals. In the years and centuries following Jesus's life, when Christianity was no longer persecuted but adopted as the official religion of the Roman Empire (313 CE), Christian theologians, influenced by Aristotle (384–322 BCE) and other philosophers, gave animals short shrift. With their emphasis on reason and belief in a hierarchy of creation, animals were considered to have no value other than serving "man." They certainly had no rights, as St. Augustine (354–430) expressed it:

> when we say Thou shalt not kill, we do not understand this of the plants, since they have no sensations, nor of the irrational animals that fly, swim, walk or creep, since they are dissociated from us by their want of reason, and are therefore by the just appointment of the Creator subjected to us to kill or keep alive for our own uses; if so, then it remains that we understand that commandment simply applying to man.

One of the most influential medieval theologians, Thomas Aquinas (1225–74), reinforced this view of animals' inferiority, taking Aristotle's stance to another level, stating that this is not just how things are but how they should be—because God had willed it. Aquinas also taught that animals are devoid of *immortal* souls. Following him and Aristotle before him, Catholic tradition did not deny, however, that they had souls; rather, they distinguished between different *types* of souls: (1) "vegetative" for vegetables, (2) "sensitive" for souls of animals, and (3) "incorporeal" (that is, rational) souls for humans. The supposed lack of rationality in plants and animals disqualified them from having immortal souls, and thus living beyond death.

This was pretty much mainstream theology on animals for centuries, but what I found intriguing was the exceptions to this view, expressed by certain mystics, visionaries, and spiritual leaders, more in touch with the heart, the intuitive, the poetic than the purely rational. (Perhaps reflective of the right side of the brain that performs tasks that have to do with creativity and the arts, while the left side of the brain performs tasks that have to do with logic and reason, such as in science and mathematics.) St. Basil the Great (330–379), a bishop from Turkey, for example, who was highly influential in founding monasticism in the East and who wrote books on the Holy Spirit expresses a more expansive view of animals in one of his prayers:

> O God, enlarge within us the sense of fellowship with all living things, our brothers, the animals, to whom you gave the earth as their home in common with us. We remember with shame that in the past we have exercised the high dominion of man with ruthless cruelty, so that the voice of the earth which should have gone up to you in song, has been a groan of travail.
> May we realize that they live not for us alone, but for themselves and for you, and that they love the sweetness of life as we do.

There are many others across the centuries from a great variety of countries who shared Basil's theology on animals. German mystic, Meister Eckhart (1260–1328), describes every creature as a "word of God," worthy to be appreciated for its potential for teaching wisdom:

> Apprehend God in all things,
> for God is in all things.
> Every single creature is full of God
> and is a book about God.
> Every creature is a word of God.

The Italian mystic St. Francis of Assisi (1181–1226), influenced by the Celtic saints' love of nature and kinship with animals, spoke of "brother sun and sister moon," preached to the birds, pacified a wolf, treated all creatures as fellow-companions on the journey of life.

Later Christian writers, such as the Russian Fyodor Dostoyevsky (1821–81) incorporated these earlier mystics' views on animals into his own works, telling his readers:

> Love all God's creation, the whole universe, and each grain of sand. Love every leaflet, every ray of God's light; love the beasts, love the plants, love every creature. When you love every creature, you will understand the mystery of God in created things.

In another part of the world, the Native American, Nicholas Black Elk (1863–1950), Oglala Lakota visionary who later, after his Catholic baptism, became a catechist and who is now being considered for sainthood, combined in his theology both his native view of the Great Spirit with his Catholic belief in the Holy Spirit:

> We should understand well that all things are the work of the Great Spirit. We should know the Great Spirit is within all things: the trees, the grasses, the rivers, the mountains, and the four-legged and winged peoples; and even more important, we should understand that the Great Spirit is also above all these things and peoples. When we do understand all this deeply in our hearts, then we will fear, and love, and know the Great Spirit, and then we will be and act and live as the Spirit intends.

John Henry Newman, an English theologian, writer, poet, and now a Catholic saint, preached a memorable sermon as an Anglican priest, before his conversion to Catholicism, in St. Mary's University Church, Oxford. He preached it on Good Friday, 1842, comparing the suffering of innocent animals to the suffering of Christ:

> consider how very horrible it is to read the accounts which sometimes meet us of cruelties exercised on brute animals. Does it not sometimes make us shudder to hear tell of them, or to read them in some chance publication which we take up? At one time it is the wanton deed of

barbarous owners who ill-treat their cattle, or beasts of burden; and at another, it is the cold-blooded and calculating act of men of science, who make experiments on brute animals, perhaps merely from a sort of curiosity. I do not like to go into particulars, for many reasons; but one of those instances which we read of as happening in this day, and which seems more shocking than the rest, is when the poor dumb victim fastened against a wall, pierced, gashed, and so left to linger out its life. Now do you not see that I have a reason for saying this, and am not using these distressing words for nothing? *For what is this but the very cruelty inflicted upon our Lord?* He was gashed with the scourge, pierced through hands and feet, and so fastened to the Cross, and there left, and that as a spectacle.

These are just a few examples from Christian history, expressing a much more positive view of animals than those who demean them in value and practice because they are supposedly not rational nor as capable as humans. (The word today for this belief is "speciesism," defined as "the assumption of human superiority leading to the exploitation of animals.") Aside from that perspective, however, as I began to teach new theology courses at St. Kates I discovered that other spiritual traditions had some of the same more positive and inclusive views of animals as did certain Christian mystics, poets, authors, and churchmen. In one honors course, entitled "Thinking About Animals: Our Kinship and Our Responsibilities," that I taught with Jeff Johnson, an animal ethicist in the philosophy department, we explored some of these different traditions. Just as not all followers in these other traditions are alike in their beliefs, as is true of Christianity, there was an underlying respect in many of them for animals. *Judaism* teaches that animals are part of God's creation and should be treated with compassion. Humans must avoid as much as possible causing pain to any living creature. Among Jewish mystics, many Kabbalists believe that animals have souls and that they go to heaven. Among *Muslims*, the sacred book of Islam, the Koran, says that "there is not a beast on earth, nor fowl that flies on two wings, but they are a people like you, and to Allah they shall return." In practice, however, dogs, in particular, are treated horribly by many Muslims. Considered unclean by the Islamic legal tradition that warns against contact with dogs, they are subject to outright abuse, cruelty or neglect. In Iran today, for example, even dog-walking has been banned from public places! Again, there is an exception to the rule (or rules). Many Muslim mystics, the Sufis, in particular, are much more friendly toward animals in general, and many are vegetarians.

Buddhism, with its belief in reincarnation teaches the need to respect every creature since humans may return in their form. Siddhartha himself is said to have had numerous rebirths in a great variety of forms, including many animals, before becoming Buddha. The Mahayan school of Buddhism teaches that animals possess Buddha nature and therefore have the potential for enlightenment. *Hinduism* has a great variety of gods, one of whom is an animal, an elephant, Ganesh, Lord of success, knowledge and wealth, who is often depicted riding a mouse that assists the deity in removing barriers to success. In India, cows are considered sacred because of their association with Lord Krishna, another of the most popular Hindu deities. To venerate them, it is believed, is to receive many personal and familial blessings as well as economic benefits. It is estimated that at least 40% of the Indian population is vegetarian. More than 5.2 million stray cows roam sidewalks in major cities as well as small villages today—as anyone can attest who has visited India.

In the West, the belief that animals are deserving of respect and recognized for their own inherent rights is something that has emerged in the past century, although its roots are traced back to the animal protection movement in Victorian England in response to the poor, if not outrageous treatment of urban workhorses and stray dogs. Today animal rights are increasingly being discussed and acted upon politically. It was not until Red's death that I began to consider this and read about it, and eventually teach about it. I remembered being in Oxford, England, in 1988, doing post-doctoral studies in Celtic spirituality, when I saw an unusual parade consisting of various animals, large and small, being led or ridden by students and others, through the streets. Inquiring what this was about, I was told it was a parade in support of animal rights—a topic I had not heard of before nor of which I had any comprehension at the time. I remember looking in amazement at who these people were and wondering what they were about! (I did, however, love seeing the animals.)

Then years later, after Red's death, I discovered the writings of Andrew Linzey, an Anglican theologian in Oxford who had begun devoting his life to animal welfare in the 1970s at the time an awareness of animal rights was growing. (He may have been the organizer of that parade!) He had gone on to write many theological books on animals and the emerging theological discipline he called "animal theology," "a theology," as he succinctly defined it, "concerned with the suffering of animals." A member of the faculty of theology at the University of Oxford, in 2006 he founded the Oxford Centre for Animal Ethics, the world's first academy dedicated to the ethical enhancement of the status of animals. Dr. Linzey is considered today *the* pioneer in the philosophical and theological promotion of animals.

Once I began reading Dr. Linzey's books (I think the first one I picked up was *Creatures of the Same God: Explorations in Animal Theology*, published the year Red died), I was drawn to reading more of them, including some for the courses I was now teaching. In August, 2012, when I was taking my son Daniel to Ireland for an introduction to his heritage, finally, I wanted to stop in England on the way back and meet with Dr. Linzey. But since the Olympics were in progress there that summer, I decided it might not be an opportune time. A year later, however, I somehow received an invitation from the Oxford Centre he founded inviting me to consider giving a paper at their first international conference, to be focused on animals and world religions, to be held in Oxford the following year, 2014. My proposal on the topic of the Celtic saints and animals was accepted, for which, of course, I was overjoyed. Not only would I get back to Oxford, one of my favorite places in the world, but to a conference *on animals*, AND the opportunity of meeting Dr. Linzey! The paper I gave was entitled "A New Ethic of Holiness: the Celtic Saints and their Kinship with Animals." The conference itself was the most interesting academic gathering I had ever attended, and, yes, I got to meet and get to know Dr. Linzey (whom I now call Andrew) and his wonderful daughter, Clair. Not only did I have the honor of sitting at the main dinner table with Andrew and Clair and their board at the closing celebration, but was asked to become a fellow at the Centre. All of this became a turning-point in the direction of my teaching and writing, and, as I began the delivery of my paper, I acknowledged, with tears, "I would never be here except for my dear dog, Red."

Continuing my friendship with both Andrew and Clair, I read more of Andrew's books, only to discover that he too believed, as I had come to believe through my readings and my muse, Red, that "the lives of the saints and St. Francis of Assisi in particular represent an alternative tradition to that of scholastic theologians." As Andrew says in *Creatures of the Same God*, they [the saints] "kept alive a more inclusive, animal-friendly vision of peaceableness and redemption at a time when the very notion that there could be friendship with animals was being derided by scholastic theologians like St. Thomas Aquinas." Andrew's writings also helped enlighten me on a clearer understanding of my vision of the two doves on the bluff that Red had led me to years before. Andrew writes how "although Christianity has a poor record on animals (as it does, it must be said, on the treatment of slaves, women, children, and gays)," something else must be considered:

> Animals have a God-given life (*nephesh* in Hebrew). This means, among other things, that each individual animal is animated by the same Holy Spirit that gives life to all creatures, humans included. This bestows on sentient life especially capacities for living—capacities for feeling, capacities for seeing—unique and distinct potentialities which must logically be valued by their Creator. God has created a multi-eyed and multi-feeling world that is, as it were, felt by the Spirit *from within*. Consider yet further: humans have "dominion" over animals. But that "dominion" (*radah* in Hebrew) does not mean despotism; rather

we are set over creation to care for what God has made
and to treasure God's own treasures.

When I read this paragraph, it was once again, like the bright
beam of light leading me, with Red's help to the icon in my study.
But this time I was taken back to the bluff on the hill and the vision
Red and I had *together* of the two doves over the waters. Taking the
Christian symbol of the Holy Spirit as a dove, the *two* doves were
perhaps teaching me of the Spirit's expression in both humans, like
me, and sentient animals, like Red. The Spirit is alive in all of creation, but perhaps most especially in animals as well as humans,
animated, as Andrew says, "by the same Holy Spirit that gives life
to all creatures," humans, and, yes, animals alike.

It took years to understand better the meaning of the two
doves, with Red at my side, Red who had led me to that bluff. If
only Ian Baker, my analyst in Zurich, was still alive for me to tell
him (but I have told him in prayer). A talented Jungian of great
depth, he would have reminded me that some of our dreams and
visions have multiple layers of meaning that sometimes take de-
cades or a lifetime to fully understand.

In another book by Andrew, I was given insight into my
question about what sort of God I had come to believe in after
my grieving the loss of Red. He explores in his book, *Christianity
and the Rights of Animals*, this union of men and animals through
the Holy Spirit discussed above. But he goes on to quote the Book
of Ecclesiastes from the Hebrew Scriptures in a text that reminds
Christians of Ash Wednesday, the beginning of Lent:

> For the fate of the sons of men and the fate of beasts is
> the same; as one dies, so dies the other. They all have the
> same breath, and man has no advantage over the beasts;
> for all is vanity. All go to one place; all are from the dust,
> and all turn to dust again.

Andrew explains in a way that echoes much of what the
Catholic theologian Elizabeth Johnson posits in her book, *Ask
the Beasts: Darwin and the God of Love*, when she speaks of God's
"deep incarnation" and "deep resurrection" which applies not only

to humans, she says, but to animals as well, precisely because God, we believe, is a God of compassion who is with all those who suffer, surely not limited to humans alone. Andrew posits an inclusive vision of both human and animal redemption:

> Notice here that it is the "same breath" of the Spirit which unites man and animals in covenant fellowship. Whatever hope there might be for a future life for humans applies equally to animal life as well. It is in this sense, and this strictly, that we can affirm (to use past language) "animal souls," though preferably we should speak of "animal redemption." We affirm the hope of future life for animals as we affirm that the Spirit is the basis of their breath; we should affirm the necessity of redemption as we ponder with the biblical writers how it is that God's moral goodness will triumph over moral evil. "If there is any sentient being which suffers pain, that being," writes Keith Ward, "must find that pain transfigured by a greater joy." It is quite impossible to posit a *loving* Creator who allows the life he has created, loved and sustained to be thrown away as worthless. "Immortality for animals, for animals as well as humans, is a necessary condition of any acceptable theodicy," concludes Ward.

In other words, if a person of Christian faith is to believe in a Creator, a God of love, one must acknowledge, and hope that such a God would not throw away the creatures, besides humankind, who share a Spirit of love and compassion. And to have such faith and hope draws one, naturally, to a life of love and compassion toward not only other sentient beings but all of creation. That is the answer, tentative, yes, but an answer to the question Red's death raised in me about what sort of God I could or would want to believe in. I believe in a God of love who most fully was revealed in the incarnation, his life, his death, and resurrection.

Which brings me back to the question that haunted me for so long, one that I asked God so often in the days after Red's death: why did she die on Good Friday, the day associated with the death of Jesus? What was that synchronicity meant to teach me?

For that answer, I found affirmation in the homily John Henry Newman gave at Oxford on *Good Friday*, 1842, when he related his horror of reading about a poor animal "fastened against a wall, pierced, gashed, and so left to linger out its life," and compares it and its suffering to Christ's own agony and death on the cross. You can only imagine my surprise when I first read that his sermon took place on that day, the day that my dear dog Red had died, and one in which Newman compares the suffering of animals to the suffering of Christ! This surprise was only reaffirmed when I came across Andrew Linzey's statement in *Why Animal Suffering Matters*: "We have failed to see the face of the Crucified in the faces of suffering animals." And he continues:

> So, if we ask . . . why should the sufferings of vulnerable, innocent, unprotected, defenceless beings be judged to be theologically significant?—the answer must be that there is something Christ-like about such suffering. It ought to compel a moral response as ought the suffering of Christ himself. We are right to be, in Newman's words, "moved" and "sickened" because that kind of suffering—whether of humans or of animals—of the innocent, unprotected, and vulnerable is morally unconscionable.

And Andrew adds:

> One further connection should be made, and it goes to the heart of the issue about Christian believing and suffering generally. Given the close correspondence between these two kinds of suffering, and their identical moral underpinning, it should follow that those who are properly sensitized to the sufferings of the crucified ought—for the same reasons—to be sensitive to the suffering of all vulnerable and innocent beings.

So why did Red die on Good Friday? Of course that ultimately remains a mystery, but for me, I believe a possible reason is to make me aware of the suffering so many animals experience daily, and to ask myself what I can do perhaps to alleviate in some small ways their pain. Red, through her patient suffering throughout Lent and then Holy Week, dying as she did, was giving an example of the passion animals suffer too, and our need to have compassion for them.

Obviously, her suffering was not like those animals confined in cages or pens at factory farms, trained or treated in abusive ways to amuse or entertain humans, used in laboratories for experimentation, killed for their fur, or even tortured horribly before they die. But Red had her own cross to bear, her own suffering those last months as she grew steadily weaker and miserable physically. Her suffering was real as she followed me around those days, lay on the floor, hoping for a cool place to rest, became more lethargic and unable to get out of her kennel, unable to climb the steps or walk very far before collapsing. But she bore her suffering patiently, as Jesus had done; she did NOT growl or bite or attack. She was gentle and patient as so many people, from vets to her groomer and others appreciated about her.

Yes, she died on Good Friday, the day Jesus died on the cross. The resurrection, of course, wouldn't have happened without Jesus's death which is why Christians call that Friday "good." Red too suffered and died on that day, but she is still very much alive for me, as my muse and source of learning, and I am grateful that she, through her life of unconditional love, gave me new life, and a new direction in mine. Now I have a better sense of her ongoing life, and the life I have with my son Dan, and the life she gave both of us. We were blessed by her presence. As JoAnne said, she was "a special dog."

"Holy Week," in retrospect, from the vantage point of grieving, truly was holy for both Red and those who loved her—a time of coming to grips with death, the agony of dying, the tears of grief and loss, and, yes, *eventually the joy of resurrection.*

Yes, Daniel, I too hate death, as you said when our Reddy died. But our faith teaches there is something greater than it. Love endures, Love overcomes the darkness and grief of death, death cannot terminate Love.

Conclusion

Cesar Millan, the famous "dog-whisperer" with his own television show, writes in his book, *Cesar's Way*, "I believe each dog comes into your life to teach you something."

This memoir has been the attempt to answer some of the deepest questions that the death of Red raised in me, as well as a way to heal some of my grief. Grieving is very much a necessary part of being human; it is our need to give voice to the love and tears inside us. I felt this need to write about her within days of her death. I have come to see that the depth of our grief will be in direct proportion to the depth of our love. The truth about this story of Red is how much my son Daniel and I loved her, and its underlying theme is how much she changed each of us for the better *through her love*. We both continue to love her fiercely, for the way she entered our lives, and for how much love and happiness she brought us and many others, including some who never knew her personally. One of my students, Nicole Sweeney, wrote a paper for a course I had taught on animals and spirituality at St. Kates, a course in which, one evening, I had invited my son, Daniel, to share his reflections on Red. Nicole entitled her paper simply "Red," of which the following is an edited version:

> Throughout the entire course, we have heard numerous stories of your dog Red. It isn't hard to see that this truly beautiful animal has taught you many things. What you might not realize is that she has also taught us many things as well. While thinking about this past semester

it became obvious that she was the inspiration for the course. She played such a large role in your life, and I was fortunate enough to be a part of the audience that you shared these stories with. Sometimes you take things for granted, and don't realize how much they meant to you until after they are gone. I don't think this was true for you; I believe that you enjoyed every second you had with her. You have said numerous times that she truly was a member of the family; this was one way that you allowed her to play a large role in your life. I believe she was also a member of the family because she helped bring you and your son Daniel together. Hearing you both talk about her made it quite clear that you had both bonded over raising her. You are also becoming closer by writing a book about her and I am inspired by that. Not every child and father are able to do that! How fun, to rediscover your love for Red together and reminisce throughout the writing process. Your relationship with Red seems like a true friendship, a true love. She brought you so much joy . . . Red has brought to my attention the importance of animals in our lives. They add a certain richness to our lives. They offer unconditional love that is unlike that of a person. They can be an addition to a family. From the many stories I can tell that Red was all of these things and much, much more. I hope to have a pet of my own like Red someday.

Nicole, of course, got an A on that paper—which I read through my tears.

As I have said here, Red was my psychopomp, my spirit guide, my muse, my soul friend leading me to new directions in my life. She was also my teacher. She teaches through my memories of her, for my memory is alive with her presence, her love. She continues to teach me many things.

One of those things is greater concern for the suffering of animals, their treatment, as well as their inherent goodness. I learned from her a heightened sense of compassion for all sensate creatures, and, yes, especially dogs and cats. I cry a lot reading about their torture and killing in China, Korea, India, Thailand,

and other parts of Asia. In China, for example, more than 10 million dogs and about four million cats are killed every year for their meat, a practice especially virulent in the annual dog meat and lychee festival in the Chinese city of Yulin. In China's southern Guangdong province alone it is estimated people eat 10,000 cats per day. In Korea, especially in rural areas, some people still believe that dogs can be eaten, and that their flesh is especially wonderful if they are tortured first and skinned alive! One million dogs are consumed per year in South Korea, although due to the efforts of the Korean Animal Rights Advocates, consumption of dog meat is less common now, particularly among younger people. Among some elderly people, however, cat soup is still popular, believed to be a remedy for neuralgia and arthritis. In India some 30,000 dogs are slaughtered for food where many believe that dog meat has medicinal value. In Thailand, a law is being considered to ban the dog meat trade, but there is still a small minority of rice farmers and day laborers who, as in Vietnam, want it to continue. But the good news is that dog lovers far outnumber dog eaters among Thailand's nearly 70 million people, and that throughout Asia the practice of eating cats and dogs has become less common as pet ownership rises, and a new generation has different attitudes to eating domestic animals. But, according to the Humane Society International (which I support, among others), an estimated 30 million dogs, including stolen family pets, still are killed across Asia every year for human consumption.

The West has its own issues, of course, where animals, especially dogs, cats, horses, cattle, chickens, and sheep are used, abused, chained, neglected, and killed. In regard to cattle, what is especially heartless is the practice of separating young calves from their mothers and placing them in wooden or metal crates, too small for them to even turn around in, for their eight-to-sixteen week lives before they are slaughtered and become "veal." Pigs, few people realize, are highly intelligent, but on factory farms, they are separated from their mothers as young as ten days old, castrated (if male), their tails chopped off and the ends of their teeth broken with pliers—without giving them any pain-killers. Often they are placed in extremely crowded pens, not unlike their mothers who are confined in "gestation" crates while pregnant where they can't turn around, and after giving birth moved to "farrowing" crates which are wide enough for them to lie down and nurse their babies but not large enough for any comfort or mobility. According to the People for the Ethical Treatment of Animals, over 100 million animals are annually killed in the United States alone. Animal experimentation on mice, rats, rabbits, monkeys, cats, and dogs and other animals is still being tolerated, including forcing rats and mice to inhale toxic fumes, dogs being force-fed pesticides, and rabbits' eyes poisoned with corrosive chemicals—all for the sake of humans' better cosmetics and supposedly better health. It is estimated that more than 115 million animals worldwide are used in laboratory experiments every year but because they are done in "research facilities" unavailable to ordinary people, few know of their suffering, languishing in pain, extreme frustration, and loneliness. Dog fighting is still a horrendous pastime for some in both urban and rural area where dogs are bred and trained from puppyhood to fight each other, often in a pit, until one or more dogs are either dead or so wounded that they cannot continue. Their audiences of onlookers or those who bet for money frequently include children who obviously learn that such cruelty is not only "entertaining" but acceptable. *Such attitudes have their effect, as is proven that intentional cruelty to animals is strongly correlated with other crimes, including violence against children, adults, and the elderly.* Puppy mills still exist in many states where puppies are often housed in wire cages, stacked on top of each other, in conditions highly unsanitary where they suffer from health and social problems. Some mills have been found to have up to a thousand dogs under one roof. Currently, while forty-six of the fifty states have now enacted felony penalties for certain forms of animal abuse, in most jurisdictions, animal cruelty is most commonly charged, if at all, as a misdemeanor offense.

Because of my love for Red and sensitivity toward her suffering, I began to read about and then connect with those people and organizations who are dedicated to the elimination of the untold suffering of so many vulnerable animals. Teaching that Honors course with Jeff Johnson, my colleague at St. Kates, and others whom I got to know through him and through my reading, I try to raise the awareness of animals' suffering whenever I can and donate money to organizations or sanctuaries caring for them or trying to stop their torture and death. I cry at stories I read on Facebook and in the newspapers of animal neglect or abuse, stories too of their abandonment as they grow older or have become an "inconvenience," especially dogs giving their trust, loyalty, and affection to humans, and then being left behind or even worse, euthanized because they're no longer wanted.

Perhaps on a deeper level than the awareness of animal suffering throughout the world and the need to prevent it is what Red taught me personally. First of all, there was the lesson of how she lived her life, how she began each day, filled with the excitement of new beginnings, new adventures, bounding from her kennel. The memory of her example reminds me how it's up to me to follow her example and nurture my own sense of wonder, whether the day begins with clouds and rain in spring or blowing snow announcing the arrival, in Minnesota, of five or six more months of it!

Most importantly, there's also what she taught me about the trials of aging, of how during the last weeks and months of her being examined, probed, her blood extracted, she never snarled, barked, or bit anyone. Her last days, huddled in her kennel or seeking to find a cool place, she suffered in silence. I'd reach in to touch her, to bless her, and she would slowly raise her head and wag her tail. Amazing grace she manifest! Through it all she taught *me* to be patient with my own suffering, the suffering that comes with aging and the diminishment of body. Patience in suffering, she reminds me, as I climb the steps more slowly. Patience in all things, Daniel says he learned from her. Patience and taking time to smell the roses. What a rich legacy!

Red was a revelation of beauty, from the first sight of her when Dan and I saw her with her siblings, on through her beauty as she aged, even in our arms when her suffering finally ended. Her physical beauty was extraordinary, but most especially her *spiritual* beauty offering constant joy and unconditional love—from her bounding from her kennel in the morning to her play in the backyard with Dan and Mel to her walks with me through the neighborhood and on up to the bluff where the doves appeared. Even just her sitting next to me in the green chair or next to Dan by the tree at Christmas were manifestations of joy shared between us and Red—beautiful moments of joy because of the beauty she manifest. My friend, John O'Donohue, the Irish poet-philosopher, writes in his book *Beauty: The Invisible Embrace* that every day "each one of us is visited by beauty," if we but take time to look, to open our eyes. Red was such a visitation to Dan and me, helping to make each day more joyful and at times more tolerable.

St. Augustine writes throughout his autobiography of his search for God, finally coming to the realization that God is love, reflected in so many ways, including the beauty of creation. In Book Ten of his *Confessions*, he addresses the heavens, the sun, the moon, the stars, asking them, "Tell me about my God, you who are not God." "And they cried out in a loud voice," he writes, 'He made us.'" And then he says, ". . . their answer was in their beauty." What for me, then, reflects the beauty of God? I ask myself in reading Augustine. My answer comes—in family, friendships, nature and its changing seasons, and in memories of my dog, Red.

Red was born beautiful and she was beautiful until the end, and after her death, looking down at her still body, I saw that beauty reflected in an astonishing way. At last no longer suffering, she seemed transfigured, as if she were a puppy again, asleep at our side. We wept, Daniel and I, at the sight of her still body, recalling how much joy she had brought into our lives, and grieving terribly that now she was gone.

Gone, but not forgotten. The dead leave our presence but they never leave our lives. Red graced our lives, and always will. She taught us, most of all, that what counts is not living long so much as living well. And living well has to do with our own love and compassion toward all creatures and all creation, especially our beloved, precious planet earth.

OUR DOG RED

Reddy died over a decade ago now, but she accompanies me daily in my thoughts and in my heart. Her grave is visible each morning when I let Hana and my other puppy, Mac, out at the crack of dawn. It is there in the shadows when I let them out again before going to bed. She taught me that animals are our fellow-creatures and not here just to be used, abandoned, or cast aside. They are, as Henry Beston says, "other nations," worthy of our respect and, in many ways, our gratitude, for the contributions they make that truly enrich our lives.

I pray that, when I die, Red will be among those loved ones, family and friends, who greet me, wagging her tail, as she always did upon my arrival, welcoming me home.

Red Moon Goddess was born July 1, 1995;
she died April 6, 2007.

Works Cited

Anderson, Allen and Linda. *Saying Good Bye to Your Angel Animals: Finding Comfort After the Loss of Your Animal Friend*. Novato, CA: New World Library, 2009.

Beston, Henry. *The Outermost House*. New York: Henry Holt and Company, 1988.

Colgrave, Bertram. *Two Lives of Saint Cuthbert*. London: Cambridge University Press, 1985.

Dostoyevsky, Fyodor. *Selected Letters*. New Brunswick, NJ: Rutgers University Press, 1987.

Doty, Mark. *Dog Years: A Memoir*. New York: HarperCollins, 2007.

Johnson, Elizabeth. *Ask the Beasts: Darwin and the God of Love*. Continuum, 2014.

Kemmerer, Lisa. *Animals and World Religions*. Oxford University Press, 2012.

Kubler-Ross, Elisabeth. *On Death and Dying*. Simon & Schuster/Touchstone, 1969.

Linzey, Andrew, and Yamamoto, Dorothy, eds. *Animals on the Agenda*. Chicago, IL: University of Illinois Press, 1998.

———. *Animal Theology*. Chicago, IL: University of Illinois Press, 1994.

———. *Christianity and the Rights of Animals*. Eugene, OR: Wipf and Stock Publishers, 1987.

———. *Creatures of the Same God: Explorations in Animal Theology*. Brooklyn. New York: Lantern Books, 2009.

———. *Why Animal Suffering Matters*. Oxford University Press, 2009.

Meister Eckhart. *Meister Eckhart, from Whom God Hid Nothing: Sermons, Writings, and Sayings*. New Seeds, 2005.

New Jerusalem Bible. Garden City, New York: Doubleday & Company, 1966.

Millan, Cesar. *Cesar's Way*. New York: Harmony Books, 2006.

Nouwen, Henri. *Life of the Beloved*. New York: Crossroad, 1992.

O'Donohue, John. *Beauty: The Invisible Embrace*. New York: HarperCollins, 2004.

Progoff, Ira. *Jung, Synchronicity, and Human Destiny: C.G. Jung's Theory of Meaningful Coincidence*. New York: Three Rivers Press, 1987.

Sellner, Edward. *Father and Son: Time Lost, Love Recovered.* Notre Dame, IN: Ave Maria Press, 1995.

———. *Step Five: Telling My Story.* Center City, MN: Hazelden Foundation, 1992.

Smith, Richard. *Saint Basil the Great.* London:Aeterna Press, 20015.

Starita, Joe. *"I Am a Man": Chief Standing Bear's Journey for Justice.* St. Martin's Press, 2008.

Steltenkamp, Michael. *Black Elk: Holy Man of the Oglala.* University of Oklahoma Press, 1993.

Sweeney, Jon. *The Complete Francis of Assisi.* Brewster, MA: Paraclete Press, 2015.

Warner, Rex, trans. *The Confessions of St. Augustine.* New York: New American Library, 1963.

Webb, Stephen. *On God and Dogs: A Christian Theology of Compassion for Animals.* Oxford University Press, 2002.

Wood, Juliette.*The Celtic Book of Living and Dying.* San Francisco: Chronicle Books, 2000.

Works Recommended

Barton, Julie. *Dog Medicine: A Memoir*. New York: Penguin Books, 2016.

Baume, Sara. *spill, simmer, falter, wither*. Boston: Mariner Books, 2015.

DeMello, Margo, ed. *Mourning Animals*. East Lansing: Michigan State University, 2016.

Harris, Julia. *Pet Loss: A Spiritual Guide*. New York: Lantern Books, 2003.

Hobgood-Oster, *A Dog's History of the World*. Waco, TX: Baylor University Press, 2014.

Horowitz, Alexandra. *Inside of a Dog*. New York: Scribner, 2009.

Linzey, Andrew. *Animals & Christianity: A Book of Readings*. Eugene, OR: Wipf and Stock Publishers, 1990.

Mac Coitir, Niall. *Ireland Animals*. Cork, Ireland: The Collins Press, 2010.

McElroy, Susan. *Animals as Teachers and Healers*. New York: Ballantine Books, 1997.

Morris, Willie. *My Dog Skip*. New York: Vintage Books, 1996.

Nicoll, Kate. *Soul Friends: Finding Healing with Animals*. Indianapolis: Dog Ear, 2005.

Oliver, Mary. *Dog Songs*. New York: Penguin Press, 2013.

Pacelle, Wayne. *The Bond: Our Kinship with Animals*. HarperCollins, 2001.

Pierce, Jessica. *The Last Walk: Reflections on Our Pets at the End of Their Lives*. University of Chicago Press, 2012.

Podberscek, Anthony, ed. *Companion Animals & Us*. Cambridge University Press, 2001.

Roberts, Holly. *Vegetarian Christian Saints: Mystics, Ascetics, & Monks*. Anjeli Press, 2004.

Rudy, Kathy. *Loving Animals: Toward a New Animal Advocacy*. Minneapolis, MN: University of Minnesota Press, 2011.

Russack, Neil. *Animal Guides in Life, Myth and Dreams*. Toronto, Canada: Inner City Books, 2002.

Safina, Carl. *Beyond Words: What Animals Think and Feel*. N.Y.: Henry Holt, 2015.

Scully, Matthew. *Dominion*. New York: St. Martin's Griffin, 2002.

Sellner, Edward. *Celtic Saints and Animal Stories: A Spiritual Kinship*. Paulist Press, 2020.

Sheldrake, Rupert. *Dogs That Know When Their Owners Are Coming Home*. New York: Crown Publishers, 1999.

Sife, Wallace. *The Loss of a Pet*. New York: Howell Book House, 2014.

Singer, Peter. *Animal Liberation: The Definitive Classic of the Animal Movement*. New York: Harper Perennial, 2009.

Tesdell, Diana Secker. *Dog Stories*. New York: Alfred A. Knopf, 2010.